GERMAN
in a week

Shirley Baldwin
and
Sarah Boas

Headway

ACKNOWLEDGMENTS

The authors and publishers are grateful to the following for supplying photographs:

Barnaby's Picture Library: cover photo, pp.14, 74
J. Allan Cash Ltd: pp. 1, 5, 10, 12, 13, 18, 21, 22, 25, 30, 31, 33, 34, 35, 38, 45, 48, 49, 50, 53, 57, 60, 64, 74
The German Tourist Board: p. 70

ISBN 0 340 42993 3

First published 1988

Second impression 1988

Copyright © 1988 Shirley Baldwin and Sarah Boas

Typeset by Gecko Limited, Bicester, Oxfordshire
Printed in Italy for Hodder and Stoughton Ltd., Mill Road, Dunton Green, Sevenoaks, by New Interlitho, Milan.

Contents

INTRODUCTION

German in a Week is a short course which will equip you to deal with everyday situations when you visit Germany, Austria or Switzerland: shopping, eating out, asking for directions, changing money and so on.

The course is divided into 7 units, each corresponding to a day of the life of George Jackson (a sports equipment salesman) and his daughter Helen during their week in Germany. Each unit begins with a dialogue, which introduces the essential language items in context. Key phrases are highlighted in the dialogues, and the phrasebook section which follows lists these and other useful phrases and tells you what they are in English.

Within the units there are also short information sections in English on the topics covered, sections giving basic grammatical explanations, and a number of follow-up activities designed to be useful as well as fun. Answers can be checked in a key at the back of the book. English–German vocabulary is listed under topic headings on pp. 77–81, followed by a German–English vocabulary list.

Pronunciation

Remember to pronounce every sound in a German word, even the final -e.

Consonants: similar to English, but:

German sound	example
ch as in *loch*:	To**ch**ter [tochter]
j as in *yet*:	**j**etzt [yetst]
qu as in *kvass*:	**Qu**elle [kveller]
s *z* (+ a vowel):	**s**ind [zind]
otherwise as *s*:	i**s**t [ist]
ß as *s*:	naß [nass]
sch as in *shop*:	**sch**on [shown]
sp *shp* (at the beginning):	**sp**ät [shpate]
st *sht* (at the beginning):	**St**adt [shtat]
v as in *fat*:	**v**ier [fear]
w as in *vain*:	**w**ie [vee]
z as in *lots*:	**Z**immer [tsimmer]

-b, -d at the end of a word: *p, t*
-ig at the end of a word: *ich*
r trilled or rolled at beginning, always sounded at end: **r**ot [rote] He**rr** [hair]

Vowels: similar to English:

German sound	example
a long, as *farm*	Tag [tark]
a short, as *hat*	danke [danker]
e long, as *day*	leben [layben]
e short, as *net*	es [ess]
i as in *pin*	ich [ich]
o long, as *so*	Brot [brote]
o short, as *pot*	komm [kom]
u long, as *boot*	gut [goot]
u short, as *put*	Mutti [mooti]
ie as in *keep*	hier [here]

Vowels with an umlaut

ä long, as *fate*	spät [shpate]
ä short, as *met*	Pässe [pesser]
ö sim. French *œil*	Öl [erl]
ü, y sim. Fr. *une*	früh [frew]
äu as in *boy*	läuft [loyft]

Diphthongs

au as in *town*	Haus [house]
eu as in *boy*	neu [noy]
ei, ai as in *fine*	mein [mine]

INTRODUCTIONS AND GREETINGS

Arrival   When arriving at a port or airport, you will find customs and passport procedures standard and easy to follow, as most information is given in English as well as German. You should check your duty-free allowance before setting out on your journey. Look out for these signs: **ZOLL** (customs), **PASSKONTROLLE** (passport control), and when crossing the border — **GRENZE** (frontier).

am Flughafen/at the airport

George Jackson and his daughter Helen (17), a student, arrive at the airport. George, a sports equipment salesman, is met by a German colleague, Ernst Fischer, while Helen is greeted by the Bauer family with whom she is staying as a paying guest.

Ernst:	Entschuldigen Sie, bitte. **Sind Sie** Herr Jackson?
George:	Ja, **mein Name ist** Jackson. Und sind Sie Herr Fischer?
Ernst:	Ja, **ich heiße** Ernst Fischer. Also, **sehr erfreut**, Herr Jackson.
Ulrike:	(approaching) **Guten Tag** — sind Sie Fräulein Helen Jackson? **Ich bin** Ulrike Bauer, und **das ist** Gisela, meine Tochter.
Gisela:	Guten Tag. **Wie geht's**?
Helen:	**Gut, danke.**

Ulrike:	Aha, hier ist Thomas. Er kommt immer zu spät.
Gisela:	(to Helen) Das ist mein Bruder, Thomas.
Ernst:	Hier ist unser Taxi, Herr Jackson. Geben Sie mir das Gepäck. (To the driver) Hotel Berlin, bitte.
Ulrike:	Thomas, ist das Auto da?
Thomas:	Ja, Mutti.
Ulrike:	Helen, ist das Ihre Reisetasche? Wo ist Ihr Koffer? Wir fahren jetzt nach Hause.

Father and daughter say goodbye to each other and arrange to meet soon.

| Ulrike: | **Auf Wiedersehen**, Herr Jackson. |
| George: | Auf Wiedersehen, Frau Bauer. |

Saying hello and goodbye   It is usual to *shake hands* when greeting people in German-speaking countries, and to say good day and goodbye on entering and leaving such places as shops and restaurants. In Southern Germany and Austria, 'Grüß* Gott' is used instead of 'Guten Tag'. Address a man as **Herr** Jackson, most women as **Frau** Bauer, a girl or very young unmarried woman as **Fräulein** Bauer. Unlike in other languages, **Herr, Frau** and **Fräulein** are not used on their own.

* Note that the German letter **ß** is pronounced as an 's'.

Introductions

Entschuldigen Sie, bitte	Excuse me, please
Verzeihen Sie	Pardon, excuse me
Sind Sie Herr/Frau/Fräulein . . .?	Are you Mr/Mrs/Miss . . .?
Ja/Nein	Yes/No
Wie ist Ihr Name?/Wie heißen Sie?	What is your name?
Ihr Name, bitte	Your name, please
Mein Name ist . . ./Ich heiße . . .	My name is . . .
Ich bin . . .	I am . . .
Sehr erfreut	Pleased to meet you

Greetings and farewells

Guten Tag	Hello/Good day
Guten Morgen	Good morning
Guten Abend	Good evening
Gute Nacht	Good night
Hallo	Hello
Wie geht es Ihnen?	How are you?
Wie geht's?	How are things?
Gut, danke	Fine, thanks
Und Ihnen?	And you?
Auf Wiedersehen	Goodbye
Bis bald	See you later

Please and thank you

Bitte/Ja, bitte	Please/Yes please
Danke	Thank you (can mean 'no thank you')
Vielen Dank/Danke schön	Many thanks/Thank you very much
Bitte schön	Don't mention it/You're welcome

USEFUL WORDS AND EXPRESSIONS

und/also!	and/well then!
das ist meine Tochter	that's my daughter
Er kommt immer zu spät	He's always too late
mein Bruder	my brother
hier ist unser Taxi/das Auto	here's our taxi/the car
Geben Sie mir das Gepäck	Give me your luggage
da	there
Ja, Mutti	Yes, Mum
Wo ist Ihr Koffer?	Where is your suitcase?
Ihre Reisetasche	your travel bag
Wir fahren jetzt nach Hause	We're going home now

the way it works

The

All nouns in German begin with a capital letter:

meine **T**ochter   my daughter   das **A**uto   the car

The word for 'the' in German varies according to whether the noun is masculine, feminine or neuter.

For a masculine noun, use **der**:   **der** Koffer   the suitcase
For a feminine noun, use **die**:   **die** Reisetasche   the travel bag
For a neuter noun, use **das**:   **das** Gepäck   the luggage

Sometimes it is possible to guess whether a noun is masculine or feminine, e.g. **der Bruder** (the brother), **die Mutter** (the mother), but in general, each noun must be learned together with its gender.

My and your

These are adjectives, and in German they vary depending on whether the noun is masculine, feminine, or neuter.

For a masculine noun, say: **mein Name** my name,   **Ihr Name**   your name
For a feminine noun, say: **meine Tochter** my daughter,   **Ihre Tochter** your daughter
For a neuter noun, say: **mein Auto** my car,   **Ihr Auto** your car

Note that **Ihr** is always written with a capital letter. Note also **unser, unsere** (our).

I, you and he (pronouns)

In German, these are **ich**, **Sie** and **er**. **Sie** is always written with a capital letter.
In the dialogue, these pronouns are used with the verb 'to be' as follows:
ich bin I am   **Sie sind** you are   **er ist** he is

Asking questions

If you want to ask a question in German, you simply turn the sentence round, as in English:

Sie sind Herr Jackson.   You are Mr Jackson   Da ist das Auto.   There is the car.
Sind Sie Herr Jackson?   Are you Mr Jackson?   Ist das Auto da?   Is the car there?

things to do

1.1   A tour operator is meeting the train at the station, and asks the following passengers if they are members of his group. Reply for them, using complete sentences.
     1   John Lowe – Entschuldigen Sie bitte, sind Sie Herr Lowe?
     2   Françoise Leclerc – Sind Sie Fräulein Dupont?
     3   Kirk Tyler – Entschuldigen Sie bitte, heißen Sie Kennedy?
     4   José Garcia – Entschuldigen Sie bitte, sind Sie Herr Garcia?
     5   Rosemary Brown — Heißen Sie Baker?
   Now he tells them his own name. What does he say?

1.2   Practise greeting the following people:
     1   Herr Schneider: Say hello and ask him how things are.
     2   Frau Schwarz: Say good morning.
     3   Herr Kohl: Say good evening, and tell him you are pleased to meet him.
     4   Fräulein Schmidt: Say good day, and ask her how she is.

1.3   Die Familie *The family*

DIE ELTERN
(The parents)
der Mann *(husband)*
der Vater *(father)*

Ludwig   Ulrike

die Frau *(wife)*
die Mutter *(Mother)*

DIE KINDER
(the children)
der Sohn *(son)*
der Bruder *(brother)*

die Tochter *(daughter)*
die Schwester *(sister)*

Thomas 19   Gisela 16

Imagine you are Karl-Heinrich Bauer, and you are explaining your relationship to other members of your family. What would you say? The first one is done for you.

1   Ludwig ist mein Vater   3   Thomas ....
2   Ulrike ist   4   Gisela ....

Now Ludwig begins to point out the members of his family, beginning: **Das ist Ulrike, meine Frau.** But Ulrike continues with the explanation. What does she say about Ludwig, Thomas, Gisela and Karl-Heinrich?

MAKING A HOTEL BOOKING

Accommodation There are many different types and categories of hotel, varying from the very basic to the luxurious, with facilities such as saunas, gyms and swimming-pools. Detailed lists can be obtained from the German, Austrian and Swiss National Tourist Offices. Booking in advance is advisable, especially in the summer, and you normally pay for the room rather than per person. You will be expected to fill out a registration form giving details of nationality, occupation, passport number, etc.
A few types of accommodation are: **Hotel garni** (bed and breakfast only); **Pension** (boarding house); **Gasthaus/Gasthof** (Country inn); **Ferien-wohnung/Appartements** (holiday apartments).
When travelling through the country, look out for the sign **ZIMMER FREI** (rooms to let) by the roadside, or go to the nearest **Fremdenverkehrsbüro** (tourist office), which will keep a list of hotels and other accommodation. In Germany, hotels and apartments may be situated in castles, stately homes and historic inns (details from the GNTO) and holidays can be taken in farmhouses. There are over 600 **Jugendherberge** (youth hostels) for members of the International Youth Hostels Association.

George Jackson is booking in at the Hotel Berlin.

George:	(to receptionist) Guten Abend. **Ich habe ein Zimmer reserviert – für eine Woche.**
Empfangsdame:	Guten Abend. Ihr Name, bitte?
George:	Mein Name ist Jackson.
Empfangsdame:	Einen Moment, bitte . . . Jackson . . . **ein Doppelzimmer, mit Bad** . . .
George:	Nein, **ein Einzelzimmer, mit Dusche!**
Empfangsdame:	Sie kommen aus Birmingham, Herr Jackson?
George:	Nein, ich komme aus London. (He shows the receptionist his booking confirmation.) **Hier ist die Bestätigung.**
Empfangsdame:	Herr Jackson aus London. Ah, das stimmt – **Zimmer acht, im Erdgeschoß. Hier ist der Schlüssel.**
George:	Danke schön.
Empfangsdame:	Bitte schön.

Booking at a hotel

Haben Sie Zimmer frei?	Do you have any rooms?
Mein Name ist . . .	My name is . . .
Ich habe ein Zimmer reserviert . . .	I have reserved a room . . .
für eine Nacht/drei Nächte	for one night/three nights
für eine Woche/zwei Wochen	for a week/two weeks
Ich möchte . . .	I would like . . .
ein Einzelzimmer	a single room
ein Doppelzimmer	a double room
ein Zimmer mit zwei Betten	a room with twin beds
mit Bad/mit Dusche	with a bath/shower
mit Toilette/mit Fernsehen	with WC/with a TV
mit Telefon/mit Balkon	with a telephone/ balcony
nach vorn/nach hinten	at the front/at the back
im Erdgeschoß	on the first floor
im zweiten Stock	on the second floor
im dritten Stock	on the third floor
Für wieviele Personen?	For how many?
Für eine Person/Für zwei Personen	For one/For two
Vollpension/Halbpension	Full board/half board
Übernachtung mit Frühstück	Bed and breakfast

PENSION
Roseneck
am Wald

HOTEL
ALTE
POST

Prices

Wieviel kostet das Zimmer?	How much is the room?
pro Nacht	for the night
Es kostet zweihundertfünfzig Mark pro Tag	It costs 250 DM a day
Einzelzimmer Zuschlag, 10,– DM	Single room supplement 10 Marks
Das ist zu teuer	That's too much
Haben Sie etwas Billigeres?	Have you anything cheaper?
Ich nehme es	I'll take it
Wollen Sie sich bitte eintragen	Please register
Hier ist die Bestätigung	Here is the confirmation
Zimmer acht, im Erdgeschoß	Room 8 on the ground floor
Hier ist der Schlüssel	Here is the key
die Mehrwertsteuer/die Kurtaxe	VAT/visitor's tax
Es tut mir leid	Sorry
Es ist kein Zimmer frei	We have no room

MAKING CONVERSATION

zu Hause/in the house

Helen Jackson is talking to Ludwig, Gisela and Thomas's father.

Ludwig: England ist sehr schön, aber das Wetter ist nicht gut! Sie wohnen in Manchester, Helen, nicht wahr?

Helen: Nein, ich wohne nicht in Manchester. **Ich wohne in London. Ich bin Londonerin.**

Ludwig: Ah, Sie sind Londonerin! Ich habe eine Kusine in London. Und Sie sind sechzehn Jahre, wie Gisela?

Gisela: (entering) Nein, Vati, sie ist siebzehn . . . Komm Helen, das Abendessen ist nun bereit.

Where are you from?

Woher kommen Sie?	Where do you come from?
Woher sind Sie?	Where are you from?
Ich komme aus England/Deutschland/ Österreich	I come from England/Germany/Austria
Ich bin aus der Schweiz/aus Amerika	I'm from Switzerland/America
Wo wohnen Sie?	Where do you live?
Ich wohne in London/München/Wien	I live in London/Munich/Vienna
Ich bin Londoner/Londonerin	I am a Londoner (male/female)

How old are you?
(For a list of numbers, see p. 77)

Wie alt sind Sie?	How old are you?
Ich bin neunzehn Jahre alt.	I am nineteen years old.

USEFUL WORDS AND EXPRESSIONS

(Einen) Moment, bitte	Just a moment	Ich habe eine Kusine in London	I have a cousin in London
das stimmt	that's right		
aber	but	Komm	Come (along)
nicht wahr?	don't you? (etc.)	Vati	Dad
England ist sehr schön	England is very nice	das Abendessen	supper
		nun	now
Das Wetter ist nicht gut	The weather is not good	bereit	ready

the way it works

a and an

In the same way as 'my' and 'your', the word for 'a'/'an' is different, depending whether the noun is masculine, feminine or neuter:

For a masculine noun, use **ein**:   **ein** Schlüssel
For a feminine noun, use **eine**:   **eine** Woche
For a neuter noun, use **ein**:   **ein** Zimmer

More pronouns

'She' is **sie**; 'we' is **wir**.

sie ist siebzehn   she is seventeen
wir haben Zimmer frei   we have rooms to let

Here is a list of the pronouns in German, used with the verb **sein** (to be):

ich bin	I am	**wir sind**	we are
Sie sind	you are	**Sie sind**	you are (plural)
er ist	he is	**sie sind**	they are
sie ist	she is		
es ist	it is		

Verbs

Two more verbs used in this unit are **kommen** (to come) and **wohnen** (to live). Many other German verbs form their endings in the same way as these:

ich **komme**	I come	wir **kommen**	we come
Sie **kommen**	you come	Sie **kommen**	you come (pl)
er/sie/es **kommt**	he/she/it comes	sie **kommen**	they come

The verb **haben** (to have) is irregular, and should be learned:

ich **habe**	I have	wir **haben**	we have
Sie **haben**	you have	Sie **haben**	you have (pl)
er/sie/es **hat**	he/she/it has	sie **haben**	they have

Negatives

To make a sentence negative, simply use **nicht**:

Das Wetter ist **nicht** gut.	The weather is not good.
Sind Sie **nicht** aus London?	Aren't you from London?
Ich wohne **nicht** in Manchester.	I don't live in Manchester.

things to do

1.4 *Booking at a hotel*
Practise booking a room at a hotel. Use **Ich möchte** (I would like):

1
4
2
5
3

1.5 The hotel receptionist is looking at the wrong day in the diary and has got muddled up. Can you put her right?

1.6 The following people are on holiday abroad. Can you tell from their car nationality plates where they come from? The first one is done for you.

1 Ulrike Bauer **D**   Sie kommt aus Deutschland.

2 George Jackson **GB**

3 Andreas Mueller **CH**

4 Fritz Stern **Ö**

5 Amy Krupnik **USA**

1.7 Wie alt sind sie? *(How old are they?)*
Practise using numbers in German by saying how old these people are. The first one is done for you.

1 Gisela Bauer (16).
  Sie ist sechzehn.
2 Peter Böhm (12).
3 Margit Springer (5).

4 Günther Mayer (14).
5 Tomas Springer (7).
6 Ursula Böhm (20).

ORDERING BREAKFAST

▶ ▶ ▶ **Breakfast** This is traditionally a fairly substantial meal, and will often consist of boiled eggs, cold meat and sliced cheese as well as bread and rolls. In larger hotels, you may also be offered muesli and yoghurt. Coffee comes with cream, and you will have to ask for fresh milk (**frisches Milch**). Breakfast is usually served from 7 to 10 a.m. in hotels.

das Frühstück/breakfast

George Jackson is ordering breakfast at the hotel.

George: **Ich möchte frühstücken**, bitte.
Kellner: Was nehmen Sie? Es gibt Spiegeleier
           mit Speck, gekochte Eier, Rühreier,
           Schinken, Käse . . .
George: **Bringen Sie mir bitte Toast, mit
           Marmelade, und ein Glas Orangensaft.**
Kellner: Ja, gerne. Trinken Sie Tee oder
           Kaffee?
George: **Haben Sie heiße Schokolade?**
Kellner: Nein, wir haben keine Schokolade.
George: Also, **eine Tasse Kaffee – ohne Sahne**, bitte.
Kellner: Sonst noch etwas?
George: Nein danke. **Das ist alles**. Ich muß Diät leben!

What's for breakfast?

der Kellner/die Kellnerin	waiter/waitress
Ich möchte frühstücken	I'd like to have breakfast
Was nehmen Sie?	What will you have?
Was wollen Sie?	What do you want?
Was möchten Sie?	What would you like?
Es gibt . . .	There is/there are . . .
Wir haben . . .	We have . . .
Bringen Sie mir . . .	Bring me . . .
Spiegeleier mit Speck	bacon and eggs
gekochte Eier/ein gekochtes Ei	boiled eggs/a boiled egg
Rühreier/Schinken/Käse	scrambled eggs/ham/cheese
Joghurt/Wurst	yoghurt/sausage
Brot/Schwarzbrot	bread/rye bread
Brötchen/Semmeln	rolls
(ein Stück) Toast	(a piece of) toast
mit Butter und Marmelade	with butter and jam
mit Apfelsinenmarmelade/Honig	with marmalade/honey
ein Glas Orangensaft	a glass of orange juice
ein Glas Grapefruitsaft	a glass of grapefruit juice
Trinken Sie Tee oder Kaffee?	Do you want tea or coffee?
Ich möchte . . .	I would like . . .
eine Tasse Tee	a cup of tea
mit Zitrone/mit Milch	with lemon/milk
ein Kännchen Kaffee	a pot of coffee
einen schwarzen Kaffee	a black coffee
eine Tasse Kaffee mit Sahne/	a cup of coffee with cream/
ohne Sahne	without cream
eine Tasse (heiße) Schokolade	a cup of (hot) chocolate
eine Tasse Mokka	a cup of mocha
Wir haben keine Schokolade	We haven't any chocolate
Sonst noch etwas?	Anything else?
Noch ein . . ., bitte	Another . . ., please
Das ist alles	That's all
Ich muß Diät leben	I'm on a diet

SHOPPING FOR FOOD AND CLOTHES

▶ ▷ **Shopping hours**   Shops are open from 8 or 9 a.m. until 6.30 on Mondays to Fridays, and until 1.30 on Saturdays (Germany and Austria). In Germany, shops are open later on the first Saturday of each month. In small towns, they may close for lunch between 1 and 3 p.m., though department stores will remain open. In Switzerland, shops shut for a half day each week. In some places, **bakeries** are open on Sundays from 10 to 12, and sell many different varieties of bread – black, brown and white. Rye bread is popular, and brown bread is more common than white.

verkaufen/shopping

Gisela Bauer wants to spend the morning at the shops.

Gisela: Fahren wir heute morgen in die Stadt, Helen. Wir haben sehr schöne Geschäfte hier in München, und **ich suche einen Rock** für eine Party am Donnerstag.

Ulrike: Vergessen Sie nicht meine Einkäufe. (Reads from list) **Ich brauche Butter**, Käse, Reis, eine Dose Sardinen, Würstchen, zwei Kilo Zwiebeln, Äpfel, Pfirsiche, ein Dutzend Eier, eine Flasche Cola . . .

Gisela: Mutti, Mutti! Wir haben nicht soviel Zeit.

Ulrike: Du findest alles im Supermarkt, meine liebe Tochter. Hier Helen, nehmen Sie die Liste.

im Kaufhaus/at the department store

Gisela and Helen arrive at the third store that morning.

Verkäuferin: Guten Morgen. Kann ich Ihnen helfen?

Gisela: Bitte, **wieviel kostet dieser Rock? Ich trage Größe 36.**

Verkäuferin: Der blaue Rock? Es tut mir leid. Wir haben nur Größe 38 oder 40.

Helen: Wie schade! Diese Kleider sind auch schön, Gisela.

Gisela: Die grünen? Ja, aber sie sind zu teuer und zu groß. (To the assistant) **Haben Sie nichts Kleineres . . . und Billigeres** – in blau?

Verkäuferin: Es tut mir leid . . .

Helen: Du bist so schlank! (Looking at her watch) Es ist spät, und ich habe Hunger. Gibt es ein Restaurant im Kaufhaus?

Gisela: Nein, wir treffen meinen Bruder Thomas im Café . . . Aber zuerst zum Supermarkt!

Shopping for food

Einkäufe machen		to go shopping
Ich brauche . . .		I need . . .
Würstchen		little sausages
zwei Kilo Zwiebeln		2 kilos of onions
Äpfel, Pfirsiche		apples, peaches
ein Dutzend Eier		a dozen eggs
eine Flasche Cola		a bottle of cola

die Butter	butter	der Reis	rice
der Käse	cheese	der Zucker	sugar
die Margarine	margarine	das Mehl	flour
das Speiseöl	cooking oil	die Kekse	biscuits
der Joghurt	yoghurt	die Teigwaren	pasta
das Ei	egg	der Bohnenkaffee	(ground) coffee

Use the following expressions when buying food:

ein Stück Kuchen	a piece of cake
eine Packung Kekse	a packet of biscuits
ein Paket Zucker	a packet of sugar
eine Packung Tee	a packet of tea
eine Dose Sardinen	a can of sardines
eine Packung Eier	a carton of eggs
eine Scheibe Schinken	a slice of ham
sechs Scheiben Salami	6 slices of salami
eine Schachtel Pralinen	a box of chocolates
eine Tafel Schokolade	a bar of chocolate
ein Brot	a loaf of bread

▶ ▶ ▶ **Measurements**   Don't forget that the metric system of weights and measures is used on the Continent:

100 g = 3.5 oz.	1 mile = 1.6 km
1 kg = 2.2 lb	8 km = 1 mile
1 litre = 1.8 pt	

ein Kilo Birnen	a kilo of pears
ein halbes Kilo Äpfel	half a kilo of apples
zwei Kilo Kartoffeln	2 kilos of potatoes
ein Pfund Karrotten	a pound of carrots
ein halbes Pfund Tomaten	half a pound of tomatoes
Hundert Gramm Käse	100 grams of cheese
Hundertfünfzig Gramm Leberwurst	150 grams of liver paté
ein Liter Milch	a litre of milk
eine Flasche Essig	a bottle of vinegar
Wieviel kostet . . .?	How much does . . . cost?
Es kostet . . . DM pro Dutzend/per Kilo	It costs . . . Marks a dozen/kilo

Die Geschäfte (shops)

das Geschäft	shop
der Markt	market
der Supermarkt	supermarket
das Einkaufszentrum	shopping centre
das Kaufhaus/	
Warenhaus	department store

Here are some common shops:

die Bäckerei	baker's
das Lebensmittel-	
geschäft	grocer's
die Fleischerei/die	
Metzgerei	butcher's
die Fischhandlung	fishmonger's
die Obst und	
Gemüsehandlung	greengrocer's
die Konditorei	cake shop
die Milchhandlung	dairy
das Delikatessen-	
geschäft	delicatessen
das Reformhaus	health food shop

die Apotheke	chemist's
die Drogerie	drugstore
der Zeitungshändler	newsagent's
das Schreibwaren-	
geschäft	stationer's
die Buchhandlung	bookshop
das Modengeschäft	dress shop
das Schuhgeschäft	shoe shop
der Damenfriseur/	ladies/gents
Herrenfriseur	hairdresser
die chemische	
Reinigung	dry cleaner's

Look out for these notices:

SELBSTBEDIENUNG	self-service
KASSE	check-out
SCHNELLKASSE	fast check-out

EINGANG	entrance
AUSGANG	exit
KEIN AUSGANG	no exit

Buying clothes

Kann ich Ihnen helfen?	Can I help you?
Was darf es sein?	What would you like?
Ich sehe mich nur um	I'm just looking
Ich suche . . .	I'm looking for . . .
Verkaufen Sie . . .?	Do you sell . . .?
Ich möchte . . . kaufen	I'd like to buy . . .

(For a full list of clothes and colours, see p. 78)

Size and price

Zeigen Sie mir bitte . . .	Could you show me . . .
Welche Größe?	What size?
Ich trage/habe Größe 36	I take size 8
Können Sie bitte meine Maße nehmen?	Can you measure me, please?
Es tut mir leid	I'm sorry
Wir haben keine . . . in dieser Größe	We have no . . . in this size
Wir haben nur Größe 38 oder 40	We only have size 10 or 12
Wieviel kostet dieser Rock?	How much does this skirt cost?
Es ist zu teuer/groß/ lang/kurz/klein/ eng	It's too expensive/big/long/short/small/ tight
Haben Sie nichts Kleineres/Billigeres?	Haven't you anything smaller/cheaper?
teuer/billig/preiswert	expensive/cheap/good value

Sizes

Women's dresses

British	8	10	12	14	16	18	20
Continental	36	38	40	42	44	46	48

Shoes

British	3	4	5	6		7	8	9
Continental	36	37	38	39–40		41	42	43

Collar sizes

British	14	14½	15	15½	16	16½	17
Continental	36	37	38	39–40	41	42	43

Decisions

Diese Kleider sind auch schön	These dresses are nice too
Ich habe die Farbe nicht gern	I don't like the colour
Ich habe lieber blau/grün	I prefer blue/green
Kann ich es anprobieren?	Can I try it on?
Das gefällt mir nicht	I don't like it
Es paßt Ihnen ausgezeichnet	It fits you perfectly
Ich nehme es	I'll take it
Sonst noch einen Wunsch?	Would you like anything else?
Kann ich eine Quittung haben?	Can I have a receipt?

USEFUL WORDS AND EXPRESSIONS

Ja, gerne	Yes, certainly
Heute morgen	this morning
Fahren wir in die Stadt	Let's go into town
Wir haben sehr schöne Geschäfte	We have very nice shops
für eine Party	for a party
Vergessen Sie nicht . . .	Don't forget . . .
Wir haben nicht soviel Zeit	We don't have much time
Du findest alles im Supermarkt	You'll find everything in the supermarket
meine liebe Tochter	my dear daughter
Nehmen Sie die Liste	Take the list
Wie schade!	What a shame!
Du bist so schlank!	You are so slim!
Es ist spät	It's late
Ich habe Hunger	I'm hungry
Wir treffen meinen Bruder im Café	We're meeting my brother in the café
Zuerst zum Supermarkt!	First, to the supermarket!

the way it works

Du

Du also means 'you' in German, but it is not used very often – only when talking to someone you know very well, children or members of the family:

Du findest alles im Supermarkt.	You find everything in the supermarket.
Du bist schlank.	You are slim.

Dein is the familiar form of 'your', and works like **ein** and **mein**.

15

Nouns in the plural

'The' in the plural is **die**. Feminine nouns in the plural often take the ending **-n** or **-en**:

eine Bluse   zwei Blus**en**   die Rechnung   die Rechnung**en**

Masculine and neuter nouns ending in **-el, -er** and **-en** often remain the same:

der Koffer   die Koffer   das Zimmer   die Zimmer
der Schlüssel   die Schlüssel   das Kissen   die Kissen

Others add an **-e**, or add an umlaut as well as an **-e**:

das Geschäft die Geschäft**e**   der Einkauf die Eink**äu**fe

However there are a great many irregular plurals in German, and these are best learned as you come across them.

Agreement of adjectives

If an adjective comes before a noun rather than after it, then the adjective takes the ending **-e** before a singular noun and **-en** before a plural noun:

Die Schokolade ist heiß.   Die heiß**e** Schokolade.   The hot chocolate.
Der Rock ist blau.   Der blau**e** Rock.   The blue skirt.
Das Kleid ist neu. (new)   Das neu**e** Kleid.   The new dress.
Die Geschäfte sind schön.   Die schön**en** Geschäfte.   The nice shops.

But note that without an article (i.e. 'the'), you say:
Schön**e** Geschäfte, dropping the **-n**.

The direct object pronoun

When a masculine word is the object of a sentence, then the word for 'the' or 'a', etc., takes an **-n** in German:

Der Rock ist blau.   Ich nehme de**n** Rock.   I'll take the skirt.
                           Ich suche eine**n** Rock.   I'm looking for a skirt.
Mein Bruder heißt   Wir treffen meine**n**   We're meeting my
  Thomas.   Bruder.   brother.

This, these

The word for 'this' in German is **dieser**. It changes in much the same way as **der**:

dieser Käse (m)   this cheese   **diese** Butter (f)   this butter
dieses Ei (n)   this egg   **diese** Kekse (pl)   these biscuits

Verbs with a vowel change

Some German verbs have a change of vowel in the part which goes with **er/sie/es**:

tr**e**ffen (to meet): er tr**i**fft   tr**a**gen (to wear, carry): sie tr**ä**gt
h**e**lfen (to help): er h**i**lft   schl**a**fen (to sleep): sie schl**ä**ft

things to do

2.1 You are with a group of tourists at a German hotel, and the only person who speaks the language. The waiter asks 'Was möchten Sie?' Order breakfast for everyone else. The first one is done for you.

1. Deidre: a boiled egg, bread rolls with butter and jam, a pot of coffee.
   Ein gekochtes Ei, Brötchen mit Butter und Marmelade, ein Kännchen Kaffee.
2. Jeremy: bacon and eggs, toast and honey, black coffee.
3. Luisa: rye bread, ham, tea with lemon.
4. Ian: orange juice, a piece of toast with marmalade, a cup of tea with milk.
5. Chantal: bread, cheese and hot chocolate.

2.2 You are out shopping to buy food for a picnic and manage to find everything you want at the same shop. Can you tell how much money you'll need?

Preise

Eier: 1,50/Packung
Milch: 1,00/Liter
Käse: 8,40/Kilo
Mehl: 1,90/Paket
Speiseöl: 1,80/Flasche
Schokolade: 1,20/Tafel
Äpfel: 2,60/Kilo

2.3 Gisela is shopping for new clothes, but nothing that Helen suggests seems to be right. Imagine you are Gisela. What would you say in German?

1. Helen: Die gelbe Bluse ist sehr modisch (fashionable).
   Gisela: [but it's too tight]
2. Helen: Ich habe die blauen Jeans gern.
   Gisela: [they're too expensive]
3. Helen: Hast du den grauen Regenmantel gern?
   Gisela: [doesn't like the colour]
4. Helen: Das rosa Sweatshirt paßt dir (fits you) ausgezeichnet.
   Gisela: [she'll take it]

ORDERING A MEAL

Eating Lunch is generally the main meal in German homes, supper being a cold meal similar to breakfast. In restaurants, dinner is served from about 6 to 9.30 p.m. (later in larger ones). Look out for the **Menü** (set menu) which usually consists of 3 courses, often starting with a filling soup. Main courses may consist of potatoes cooked in a variety of different ways, vegetables and meat. Pork is popular in Germany, lamb is less so and shellfish are not common. There are hundreds of varieties of sausage (**Wurst**), as well as smoked meats and pickled fish. Most cities have many foreign restaurants, such as Chinese, Greek and Italian.

Restaurant bills normally include VAT and 10% service (**Bedienung Inbegriffen**), but it is usual to round up the amount, or leave a small tip.

im Restaurant/at the restaurant

George Jackson has a free evening after the opening of the Sports Exhibition. Ulrike and Ludwig Bauer have invited him to eat at a restaurant.

Ulrike:	**Hier ist ein Tisch für drei Personen**, am Fenster.
Kellnerin:	(approaching) Bitte schön, meine Damen und Herren?
Ulrike:	**Die Speisekarte, bitte, und die Weinkarte.**

Kellnerin:	Gerne. (Handing the menu) Ich empfehle Ihnen die Frikadellen, unsere Spezialität. Sie schmecken sehr gut.
Ludwig:	Einen Moment, bitte. **Gibt es ein Tagesgedeck?**
Kellnerin:	Nein, nicht am Abend.

SPEISEKARTE

VORSPEISEN	Russische Eier	egg mayonnaise
	Wurstplatte	assorted cold meat
SUPPEN	Hühnerbrühe	chicken broth
	Nudelsuppe	noodle soup
FLEISCHSPEISEN	Kalbsbraten mit Salzkartoffeln	roast veal with boiled potatoes
	Frikadellen mit Butterreis	meatballs with buttered rice
	und gemischtem Salat/	and mixed salad/
	oder Gemüse	or vegetables
	Filetsteak mit Pommes Frites	steak and chips
FISCHGERICHTE	Gebackene Forelle mit Pilzen	baked trout with mushrooms
	Panierte Scholle mit	breaded plaice with
	Petersilienkartoffeln	parsley potatoes
NACHTISCH	Käsekuchen	cheesecake
	Obsttorte	fruit flan
	Schokoladeneis	chocolate ice cream

Kellnerin:	Möchten Sie bestellen?
Ludwig:	Hmm, Ulrike. Was nimmst du?
Ulrike:	**Ich möchte** Nudelsuppe, **und dann** Frikadellen.
Ludwig:	**Ich mag keine Suppe**. Russische Eier und Kalbsbraten **für mich**.
	Na George, was essen Sie gern – Fleisch oder Fisch?
George:	**Ich hätte gern** Filetsteak mit Pommes Frites. Keine Vorspeise für mich!
Kellnerin:	Also, gut. Und zum trinken, meine Damen und Herren?
Ulrike:	**Bringen Sie uns bitte eine Flasche Weißwein**, – Rheinwein.
George:	Entschuldigen Sie, ich trinke nicht so gern Wein. Ich trinke lieber ein Glas Bier.
Ludwig:	Ich auch – **zweimal Bier**, bitte, und **ein Glas Wein** für meine Frau.
Ulrike:	(To George) Essen Sie gern Torte, George? Die Obsttorte ist hier ausgezeichnet.
George:	Oh ja! Aber **ich esse lieber** Käsekuchen.
Ludwig:	Wie Thomas. Er nimmt immer Käsekuchen.
Ulrike:	Mit Schlagsahne!

Getting a table

Haben Sie einen Tisch für drei Personen?	Do you have a table for three?
am Fenster/auf der Terrasse/ in der Ecke	by the window/on the terrace/in the corner
Ich möchte einen Tisch reservieren	I'd like to reserve a table

Ordering

Bitte schön, meine Damen und Herren?	What would you like (ladies and gentlemen)?
Die Speisekarte und die Weinkarte	The menu and the wine list
Gibt es ein Tagesgedeck?	Is there a menu of the day?
ein Touristen-Menü?	a tourist menu?
Ich empfehle Ihnen . . .	I recommend . . .
Sie schmecken sehr gut	They taste very good
Möchten Sie bestellen?	Would you like to order?
Was nimmst du?	What will you have?
Was essen Sie gern – Fleisch oder Fisch?	What would you like, meat or fish?
Was für Gemüse gibt es?	What sort of vegetables are there?
Gibt es vegetarische Gerichte?	Are there any vegetarian dishes?
Ich nehme eine Portion Bohnen	I'll have a portion of beans
Ich hätte gern/ich möchte/ich esse gern . . .	I'd like . . .
Ich mag/ich mag kein/e/en . . .	I like/don't like . . .
Keine Vorspeise für mich	No starter for me
Einmal das Gedeck	One set meal

Ordering drinks

Und zum trinken?	And to drink?
Bringen Sie uns eine Flasche Weißwein/ Rheinwein	Bring us a bottle of white wine/Rhine wine
Ich trinke nicht so gern Wein	I'm not very fond of wine
Ich trinke lieber ein Glas Bier	I'd rather have a glass of beer
Zweimal Bier	Two beers

Desserts

Dreimal Schokoladeneis	Three chocolate ices
Die Obsttorte ist ausgezeichnet	The fruit flan is excellent
Ich esse lieber Käsekuchen	I prefer cheesecake
Mit Schlagsahne	With whipped cream
Wo sind die Toiletten, bitte?	Where are the toilets?
Fräulein/Herr Ober!	Waiter/waitress!
Die Rechnung, bitte	The bill, please
Ist Bedienung inbegriffen?	Is service included?
Extraaufschlag	extra (charge)
Mehrwertsteuer	VAT
das Trinkgeld	tip
Guten Appetit!	Bon appétit!

FOOD, DRINK AND SNACKS

Understanding the menu

(*Different types of food are listed on page 79*)
The words for German dishes are often a mixture of several terms. In order to understand a menu, it is useful to know a few cooking expressions:

gebacken	baked	**gegrillt**	grilled
geräuchert	smoked	**gekocht**	boiled
gedämpft	steamed	**gefüllt**	stuffed
gebraten	fried/roasted	**überbacken**	au gratin

Die Würste (sausages)

die Weißwurst	veal and bacon sausage	**die Frankfurter**	frankfurter
		die Blutwurst	black pudding
die Zungenwurst	blood sausage	**die Wienerli**	Viennese frankfurter

Der Nachtisch (dessert)

das Eis	ice cream
das Vanillen/Zitronen/ Schokoladeneis	vanilla/lemon/ chocolate ice
der Apfelstrudel	apple strudel
Schwarzwälder Kirschtorte	Black Forest gateau
der Obstsalat	fruit salad
das Kompott	stewed fruit
Gugelhupf	raisin and almond cake
die Sachertorte	chocolate gateau
der Eisbecher	ice cream sundae
Pfirsich Melba	peach melba
Pfannkuchen	pancakes
Apfelkuchen	apple cake
die Torte/der Kuchen	tart/cake

There are many national and regional specialities in Germany, Austria and Switzerland.

Die Getränke (drinks)

ein Glas Bier (n)	a glass of beer	**eine Flasche Sekt**	a bottle of sparkling wine
ein Bier vom Faß	draught beer		
ein helles Bier	light ale	**ein Kognak (m)**	brandy
ein dunkles Bier	dark ale	**ein Likör (m)**	liqueur
ein Altbier	bitter	**ein Glühwein (m)**	mulled wine
ein Pilsener	lager	**ein Wodka (m)**	vodka
ein Glas Wein (m)	a glass of wine	**ein Whisky (m)**	whisky
eine Karaffe Wein	a carafe of wine	**ein Portwein (m)**	port
der Rotwein	red wine	**ein Apfelwein (m)**	cider
der Weißwein	white wine	**ein Kirschwasser (n)**	cherry brandy
der Rosé	rosé	**ein Schnaps (m)**	schnapps
trocken/süß	dry/sweet	**ein Glas Wasser (n)**	a glass of water

Cafés and snacks Coffee and cakes (*Kaffee und Kuchen*) are served between 3 and 5 p.m. in a **Café (Kaffeehaus** in Austria) or tea-room attached to a **Konditorei**. There are many varieties of delicious cakes, often filled with cream and liqueurs, to choose from. Cafes and bars are open all day, and sell alcoholic as well as non-alcoholic drinks, tea, coffee, etc. Cafes normally have waiter service, and price lists of drinks are displayed in the window. Look out for the **Bierstube** (similar to a pub) and **Weinstube** (wine bar). For snacks, go to an **Imbißstube** (snack bar) or **Bratwurststand** (sausage stall), where you can get rolls filled with fresh, smoked and spiced sausage, other fillings and potato salad, as well as soft drinks.

Ich habe Hunger; ich habe Durst (I'm hungry/thirsty)

Of course, you might not want to order a full meal. Here are some common snacks.

ein Sandwich (m)	sandwich	eine Zervelat-	saveloy
ein Schinkenbrot (n)	ham sandwich	wurst	
ein Käsebrötchen (n)	cheese roll	ein (deutsches) Beefsteak (n)	hamburger
		ein Halbes	
ein Omelett (n) mit Schinken/ Käse/Pilzen	ham/cheese/ mushroom omelette	Hähnchen	½ chicken
		Matjeshering (m)	salt herring
		Heringsalat (m)	herring salad
Käseschnitte (f)	cheese on toast	Kartoffelsalat	potato salad
Kartoffelchips	crisps	Strammer Max	smoked ham and
Pommes Frites	chips		fried eggs on
eine Pizza	pizza		bread
eine Bratwurst	pork sausage	ein Schaschlik (m)	shashlik
eine Frankfurter	frankfurter	DURCHGEH-	24-hour service
eine Bockwurst	large frankfurter	ENDER	
eine Currywurst	curried sausage	DIENST	

Kalte Getränke (cold drinks)

eine Flasche . . .	a bottle of
ein Glas . . .	a glass of
zwei Glas . . .	two glasses of
eine Tasse . . .	a cup of
vier Tasse . . .	four cups of
eine Limonade	lemonade
eine Cola	cola
ein Mineralwasser (n)	mineral water
ein Orangen- sprudel (m)	orangeade
ein Fruchtsaft	fruit juice
ein Apfelsaft	apple juice
ein Traubensaft	grape juice
ein Tomatensaft	tomato juice
ein Eistee	iced tea
ein Glas Milch	glass of milk
ein Bananenshake	banana milk shake
ein Ananasshake	pineapple shake

the way it works

Es gibt

The expression **es gibt** means 'there is'/'there are' and is followed by a noun as object: Gibt es ein**en** Tisch am Fenster?   Is there a table by the window?

Kein

If you want to say you haven't got something, or you don't want something, and so on, then you use **kein**. It works in the same way as **ein**:

Eine Vorspeise für Ludwig.	A starter for Ludwig.
Keine Vorspeise für George.	No starter for George.
Wir haben ein Tagesgedeck.	We have a menu of the day.
Wir haben **kein** Tagesgedeck.	We don't have a menu of the day.
Haben Sie einen Tisch frei?	Do you have a table free?
Wir haben **keinen** Tisch frei.	We haven't got a table free.
Gibt es heute Birnen?	Are there any pears today?
Nein, es gibt **keine** Birnen.	No, there aren't any pears.

Pronouns as objects

'Me' and 'him' are objects of the sentence:
I see him   Ich sehe **ihn**
He sees me   Er sieht **mich**
In German, pronouns take the object (or accusative) case after the preposition **für**.
Use these expressions in German to say 'for me', 'for him', etc.:

für mich	for me	**für uns**	for us
für Sie	for you	**für Sie**	for you (pl)
für dich	for you (fam.)		
für ihn/sie/es	for him/her/it	**für sie**	for them

Some more verbs

Here are some more common verbs you have met in this unit:

nehmen *to take*

ich **nehme**	I take	wir **nehmen**	we take
Sie **nehmen**	you take	Sie **nehmen**	you take (pl.)
du **nimmst**	you take (fam.)		
er/sie/es **nimmt**	he/she/it takes	sie **nehmen**	they take

geben *to give*

ich **gebe**	I give	wir **geben**	we give
Sie **geben**	you give	Sie **geben**	you give
du **gibst**	you give		
er/sie/es **gibt**	he/she/it gives	sie **geben**	they give

essen *to eat*

ich **esse**	I eat	wir **essen**	we eat
Sie **essen**	you eat	Sie **essen**	you eat
du **ißt**	you eat		
er/sie/es **ißt**	he/she/it eats	sie **essen**	they eat

Some German verbs add an **e** before the final **t** in the part which goes with **er/sie/es**: arbeiten (to work) – er arbeit**e**t; finden (to find) – sie find**e**t; kosten (to cost) – es kost**e**t; senden (to send) – er send**e**t.

The imperative

If you are telling someone to do something or giving someone an order, then you are using the Imperative. In German, this is very easy:

Bringen Sie mir ein Glas Bier!   Bring me a glass of beer!
Nehmen Sie das Gepäck!   Take the luggage!
Vergessen Sie nicht meine Einkäufe!   Don't forget my shopping!
Gisela, **vergiß nicht** meine Einkäufe!   Gisela, don't forget my shopping!

things to do

2.4   Ich habe keinen Hunger
A colleague, Dieter, wants to go out to a restaurant, but you are not feeling very hungry. See if you can put your preferences into German:

1 Dieter: Ich esse gern ein Filetsteak mit Kartoffeln und gemischtem Salat. Und Sie?
                 [Say you'd rather have a ham sandwich and crisps.]

2 Dieter: Ich esse gern gebackene Seezunge mit Pellkartoffeln und Pilzen. Und Sie?
                 [Tell him you'd prefer a cheese omelette and chips.]

3 Dieter: Ich hätte gern Eisbein, Knödel und Karotten. Sie nicht?
                 [Say you'd rather eat a hamburger and potato salad.]

4 Dieter: Ich esse gern ein Wiener Schnitzel mit Pommes Frites und Erbsen, und dann einen großen Eisbecher! Sie auch?
                 [Say no, you'd rather have a curried sausage.]

2.5   Und zum trinken?
You are ordering drinks at a cafe for a group of German friends. Point to each in turn, saying what he/she would like, e.g.

Ingrid: **für sie, ein Glas Traubensaft**

1 Heinz: **5** Gudrun:

2 Christa: **6** Klaus:

3 Kerstin and Norbert: **7** Hartmut and Bernd:

4 Jürgen

ASKING AND GIVING DIRECTIONS

City Transport   There are underground systems (**die U-Bahn**) in ten
German cities, and some have suburban networks (**die S-Bahn**). Tickets
for both are normally bought from automatic machines and may have to be
punched to validate (**FAHRKARTEN ENTWERTEN**) before boarding.
Tram tickets can be purchased at tram stops. You may be able to buy a
Mehrfahrkarte (a ticket valid for up to five journeys) or a daily 'rover' for
unlimited travel, and the same tickets can normally be used on
underground, trams and buses for journeys in one direction.

fahren mit der U-Bahn/taking the underground

George Jackson is setting off early in the morning to the trade fair. He asks
a passer-by for directions.

George: Entschuldigen Sie bitte. Ich besuche das Messegelände. **Wie
komme ich am besten zu** . . . uh . . . (looks at his instructions) der
Theresienhöhe?
Passant: Wie, bitte? Die Theresienhöhe? (Thinks) Von hier fahren Sie am
besten mit der U-Bahn. Die nächste Station ist Marienplatz.
George: **Wo ist das?**
Passant: Gehen Sie hier die Straße entlang, und dann links in die
Residenzstraße – das ist die dritte Straße links, glaube ich. Die
U-Bahnstation ist ungefähr nach zweihundert Metern, auf der
rechten Seite.

George: (looking bemused) Auf der rechten Seite?

Passant: Ah, Sie haben einen Stadtplan. Zeigen Sie mir – wir sind hier, Maximilianstraße; hier ist der Marienplatz, und hier ist die U-Bahnstation Messegelände.

George: Ja, ich verstehe. Sagen Sie mir, **muß ich umsteigen**?

Passant: Ja. Sie müssen im Hauptbahnhof umsteigen, und dann haben Sie nur zwei Stationen. Sie sind bald dort.

George: Und wie komme ich in die Ausstellung?

Passant: Die Ausstellungshalle ist genau gegenüber.

George: Vielen Dank.

Passant: Bitte schön.

How do I get there?

Wie komme ich am besten . . .	What's the best way to get . . .
in die Mozartstraße	to Mozartstraße
nach Stuttgart	to Stuttgart
zum Bahnhof	to the station
zum Flughafen	to the airport
zur Theresienhöhe	to Theresienhöhe
zur Universität?	to the university?

Asking for and understanding instructions

Ist das der richtige Weg zum Hafen?	Is that the right way to the harbour?
Ich suche den Dom	I'm looking for the cathedral
Wo ist . . .?	Where is . . .?
Wo finde ich . . .?	Where do I find . . .?
Wie weit ist das?	How far is that?
Es ist ungefähr noch zweihundert Meter	It's about 200 metres (to go)
Es ist nach zweihundert Metern auf der rechten Seite	It's 200 metres on the right-hand side
Sie müssen zurück	You must go back
Es ist nah/weit	It's near/far
Gehen Sie hier die Straße entlang	Go down the street
Gehen Sie geradeaus	Go straight on
Dann links/rechts in die Residenzstraße	Then left/right into Residenzstraße
Gehen Sie wieder rechts	Go right again
Nehmen Sie die zweite Straße links/die dritte Straße rechts	Take the second street on the left/ third on the right.
gleich rechts/links	immediately on the right/left

26

da drüben/gegenüber	over there/opposite
bei der Kreuzung/Ampel	at the crossroads/lights
um die Ecke	at the corner
hinter dem Postamt	behind the post office
neben der Kirche	near the church
nicht weit von . . . entfernt	not far from . . .
Die Polizeiwache liegt auf der linken Seite	The police station is on the left

Finding somewhere on a map

Sie haben einen Stadtplan	You have a map
Wir sind hier, und hier ist . . .	We're here, and here is . . .
Sie sind bald dort	You'll soon be there
Sie sind in zehn Minuten dort	You'll be there in 10 minutes
Die Ausstellungshalle ist genau gegenüber	The exhibition hall is right opposite
zu Fuß gehen	to go on foot
Ich will zum Zoo gehen	I want to go to the zoo
Zum Zoo ist es zu weit	It's too far to the zoo
Wir können zu Fuß in den Park gehen	We can go to the park on foot
der Fußgänger/die Fußgängerzone	pedestrian/pedestrian precinct

Travelling by public transport

Von hier fahren Sie am besten . . .	From here it's best to go . . .
mit der U-Bahn/S-Bahn	by tube/suburban railway
mit der Straßenbahn/mit dem Bus	by tram/by bus
mit dem Zug/mit dem Auto	by train/by car
(fliegen Sie) mit dem Flugzeug	by plane

On the underground

Wo ist die nächste U-Bahnstation?	Where is the nearest tube station?
Die nächste Station ist Marienplatz	The next station is Marienplatz
Können Sie mir zeigen?	Can you show me?
Muß ich umsteigen?	Do I have to change?
Sie müssen im Hauptbahnhof umsteigen	You have to change at the main railway station
Sie haben Umsteigemöglichkeiten . . .	There are connections . . .
in Richtung	in the direction of
Dann haben Sie nur zwei Stationen	Then you've only got 2 stations
einsteigen/aussteigen	to get on/off

USEFUL WORDS AND EXPRESSIONS

Ich besuche das Messegelände	I'm visiting the fair ground
die Messe	fair
Zeigen Sie mir	Show me
Ja, ich verstehe	Yes, I understand
Sagen Sie mir	Tell me
die Ausstellung	the exhibition

the way it works

Some more verbs

müssen *to have to, must*		**können** *to be able to, can*	
ich **muß** *I must*	wir **müssen**	ich **kann** *I can*	wir **können**
du **mußt**	Sie **müssen** (pl.)	du **kannst**	Sie **können**
Sie **müssen**		Sie **können**	
er/sie/es **muß**	sie **müssen**	er/sie/es **kann**	sie **können**

fahren *to go, drive*			
ich **fahre**	I go	wir **fahren**	we go
du **fährst**	you go	Sie **fahren**	you go (pl.)
Sie **fahren**	you go		
er/sie/es **fährt**	he/she/it goes	sie **fahren**	they go

Word order

You will have noticed in the dialogue that the order of words is not always the same as in English.

1   In German, the verb must always be the second idea in any sentence. Therefore, if something other than the subject comes first, the verb is turned round so that it will still be in second place:

Sie fahren mit der U-Bahn *but* Von hier **fahren Sie** mit der U-Bahn.

2   When a sentence contains a verb followed by a second verb in the infinitive, then the infinitive goes to the end:

Sie **müssen** im Hauptbahnhof **umsteigen**. You have to change at the main station.

Verbs of motion

If you are talking about going to or from somewhere, then you will be using a verb of motion. **In** after a verb of motion is followed by **der/die/das** in the object case. (Note that you use **gehen** when going somewhere on foot, and **fahren** when using some kind of transport.)

Ich gehe in den Park (m.)   I'm going into the park

Mit, zu, in

You will have seen how **der/die/das** change after such words as **mit** (with), **zu** (to, towards) and **in** (in, at, into). This is how it works:

der Zug (m)	**mit dem** Zug	
das Taxi (n)	**mit dem** Taxi	
die U-Bahn (f)	**mit der** U-Bahn	

der Taxistand (m)	**zum** (zu + dem) Taxistand	
das Kino (n)	**zum** (zu + dem) Kino	
die Haltestelle (f)	**zur** (zu + der) Haltestelle	

der Bahnhof (m)	**im** (in + dem) Bahnhof	in the station
das Museum (n)	**im** (in + dem) Museum	in the museum
die Kirche (f)	**in der** Kirche	in the church

However, if you are going *into* the station, museum or church, then you would be using a verb of motion, and **in** would be followed by the object case.

things to do

3.1 Here are the names of some places you will find useful when asking for or giving someone else directions:

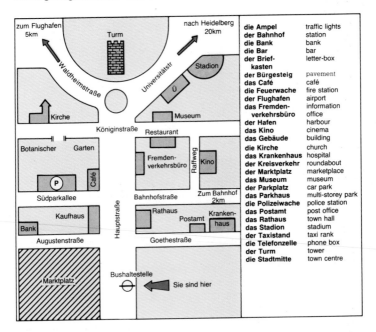

die Ampel	traffic lights
der Bahnhof	station
die Bank	bank
die Bar	bar
der Brief-kasten	letter-box
der Bürgersteig	pavement
das Café	café
die Feuerwache	fire station
der Flughafen	airport
das Fremden-verkehrsbüro	information office
der Hafen	harbour
das Kino	cinema
das Gebäude	building
die Kirche	church
das Krankenhaus	hospital
der Kreisverkehr	roundabout
der Marktplatz	marketplace
das Museum	museum
der Parkplatz	car park
das Parkhaus	multi-storey park
die Polizeiwache	police station
das Postamt	post office
das Rathaus	town hall
das Stadion	stadium
der Taxistand	taxi rank
die Telefonzelle	phone box
der Turm	tower
die Stadtmitte	town centre

You are at the bus stop on the map and overhear a German lady giving these directions to three passers-by. Look at the map. Can you tell where they want to go?

1 Gehen Sie hier die Straße entlang, dann rechts in die Königinstraße, und Sie sehen es gleich links.

2 Sie gehen geradeaus, dann die erste Straße links. Er liegt auf den rechten Seite, um die Ecke.

3 Nehmen Sie die erste Straße rechts, und es ist links, neben dem Postamt.

3.2 A number of German visitors at your hotel in Goethestraße are puzzling over the best way of getting to various places. How would you advise them? The first one is done for you.

1 Wie komme ich am besten zum Bahnhof?   Sie fahren am besten mit dem Bus.

2 . . . in die Königinstraße?

3 . . . zum Flughafen?

4 . . . nach Heidelberg?

5 . . . zur Universität?

6 . . . zum Krankenhaus?

TRAVELLING BY BUS

Bus and taxi   Buses tend to be local only, and tickets can be bought when boarding, or from automatic vending machines. However, there are a few long-distance coach services, mainly on tourist or scenic routes (e.g. **Deutsche Touring**).

Taxis are all metered. You can get a taxi from a rank (**Taxistand**) or by telephoning a **Taxizentrale**. It is usual to tip taxi-drivers, and in large cities, drivers are accustomed to giving foreign business travellers a receipt (**eine Quittung**) from which VAT can be reclaimed.

ein Tag in München/a day in Munich

Ulrike Bauer has been taking Helen round some of the sights of Munich, together with Gisela and Karl-Heinrich.

Ulrike:	Es gibt hier in München noch viel zu sehen, Helen – das Deutsche Museum, das Bayerische Museum, die Frauenkirche, die Heiliggeistkirche . . .
Gisela:	(groaning) In London hat man auch Museen und Kirchen, Mutti!
Ulrike:	(looking at her watch) **Es ist schon ein Uhr** – essen wir unser Picknick . . . Wir haben auch herrliche Parks, Helen. Der Englische Garten ist sehr schön, und der Olympiapark ist interessant.

Karl-Heinrich:	Ich will zum Zoo gehen.
Ulrike:	Nein, Liebchen, zum Zoo ist es zu weit. Aber wir können zu Fuß in den Park gehen.
Gisela:	Wir sind so müde. Hier ist eine Bushaltestelle, da drüben: nehmen wir den Bus. **Welcher Bus fährt zur Universität**, Mutti?
Ulrike:	Wir brauchen die Linie achtzehn. Aha, hier kommt unser Bus. Schnell, meine Kinder!

The time

Wieviel Uhr ist es?	What time is it?
Wie spät ist es?	What time is it?
Es ist zwei Uhr	It's two o'clock
Es ist fünf Minuten nach zwei	It's five minutes past two
Es ist viertel nach zwei	It's a quarter past two
Es ist zwanzig nach zwei	It's twenty past two
Es ist fünf vor halb drei	It's twenty-five past two
Es ist halb drei	It's half past two
Es ist fünf nach halb drei	It's twenty-five to three
Es ist viertel vor drei	It's a quarter to three
Es ist zehn vor drei	It's ten to three
Es ist drei Uhr	It's three o'clock
vormittags/nachmittags	in the morning/afternoon
abends/nachts	in the evening/at night
Es ist Mittag/Mitternacht	It's midday/midnight

Note that in German, **halb drei** (half three) is used for 'half past two'. 'Half past three' would be **halb vier**, and so on; **halb eins** = half past twelve; **ein Uhr** = one o'clock.

The twenty-four hour clock is used when referring to train timetables, etc.:

Um wieviel Uhr fährt der Zug ab?	What time does the train leave?
Um wieviel Uhr kommt der Bus an?	What time does the bus arrive?
Um vierzehn Uhr zehn	At 14.10
Der Zug fährt um siebzehn Uhr fünfunddreissig	The train goes at 17.35

Useful expressions of time

vorgestern	the day before yesterday
vor drei Tagen	3 days ago
gestern/heute/morgen	yesterday/today/tomorrow
übermorgen	the day after tomorrow
heute morgen	this morning
heute nachmittag	this afternoon
heute abend	this evening
morgen früh	tomorrow morning
jeden Tag/jede Woche	every day/every week

Taking a bus

Nehmen wir den Bus	Let's take the bus
Hier ist eine Bushaltestelle	Here's a bus stop
Gibt es eine Bushaltestelle in der Nähe?	Is there a bus stop nearby?
Wann gehen die Busse nach . . .?	When do the buses/coaches go to . . .?
Welcher Bus fährt nach Bremen/zur Universität?	Which bus goes to Bremen/to the University?
Fährt dieser Bus nach Koblenz?	Is this bus going to Koblenz?
Sie brauchen die Linie sechsunddreißig	You need a number 36
Wo muß ich aussteigen?	Where do I get off?
Bitte aussteigen!	All change!

USEFUL WORDS AND EXPRESSIONS

Es gibt noch viel zu sehen	There's still a lot more to see
das Deutsche Museum/das Bayerische Museum	the German Museum/the Bavarian Museum
die Frauenkirche/die Heiliggeistkirche	the Church of Our Lady/the Church of the Holy Ghost
In London hat man auch Museen und Kirchen	They have museums and churches in London too
Es ist schon ein Uhr	It's one o'clock already
Essen wir unser Picknick	Let's eat our picnic
Der Englische Garten ist sehr schön	The English Garden is splendid
Der Olympiapark ist interessant	The Olympic Park is interesting
Ich will zum Zoo gehen	I want to go to the zoo
Liebchen/Liebling	darling
Wir sind so müde	We're so tired
Schnell, meine Kinder	Quick, children

TRAVELLING BY TRAIN

in der Schalterhalle/at the booking office

Günther, a friend from Stuttgart, is coming to visit Thomas Bauer in Munich. He buys a rail ticket.

Schalterbeamtin:	Bitte schön?
Günther:	Guten Tag! **Eine Fahrkarte nach München**, bitte.
Schalterbeamtin:	Einmal nach München . . . einfach, oder hin und zurück?
Günther:	**Hin und zurück. Was macht das**, bitte?
Schalterbeamtin:	Zweite Klasse . . . das macht sechzig Mark und fünfzig Pfennig.
Günther:	**Wann fährt der nächste Zug** nach München?
Schalterbeamtin:	Der nächste Zug fährt um vierzehn Uhr zehn.

Günther:	**Von welchem Gleis?**
Schalterbeamtin:	Das weiß ich nicht. Normalerweise von Gleis drei oder vier. Sie müssen das Anschlagbrett lesen.
Günther:	**Muß ich umsteigen?**
Schalterbeamtin:	Nein, nein . . . (shaking her head) Was für ein ängstlicher junger Mann!
Günther:	(reading the notice board) **D-Zug nach München**, vierzehn Uhr zehn, Abfahrt Gleis fünf. (looking at his watch) Es ist nun fünf Minuten nach zwei – ich habe keine Zeit . . .
Schalterbeamtin:	Doch, Sie haben gerade noch Zeit!

Travelling by train

die Schalterbeamtin	booking office clerk (female)
Eine Fahrkarte/ein Fahrschein nach München, bitte	A ticket to Munich, please
Einfach, oder hin und zurück?	Single or return?
eine Einzelfahrkarte	a one-way (single) ticket
eine Rückfahrkarte	a return ticket
erste Klasse/zweite Klasse	first/second class
Was macht das?	What does that come to?
Wann fährt der nächste Zug nach München?	When is the next train to Munich?
Der nächste Zug fährt um vierzehn Uhr	The next train is at 14.00
Kann ich einen Sitzplatz reservieren?	Can I reserve a seat?
Von welchem Gleis?	From which platform?
Normalerweise von Gleis drei	Usually from platform 3
Sie müssen das Anschlagbrett lesen	You'll have to read the noticeboard
D-Zug nach München, Abfahrt Gleis fünf	Fast train to Munich, departure from platform 5
Muß ich umsteigen?	Do I have to change?

Das weiß ich nicht	I don't know
Was für ein ängstlicher junger **Mann**	What an anxious young man
Ich habe keine Zeit	I haven't got time
Doch, Sie haben gerade noch Zeit!	Yes, you've just got time!

Rail travel In the Federal Republic of Germany, this is run by the **Deutsche Bundesbahn (DB)**, and is generally fast, clean and very punctual. There are numerous fare reductions and schemes such as the **DB Tourist Card** for foreign visitors, or the **Tourenkarte** (available in Germany) which allows ten days' unlimited travel plus other savings. There are travel cards or reduced rates (**Sparpreisen**) for students, families, groups and pensioners, so it is worth making enquiries from the National Tourist Office.

Tickets can be bought at automatic machines for short journeys. Inter-city trains run every hour or two, and all long-distance trains have restaurant or buffet facilities. Beds or couchettes on overnight trains should be reserved, and seats are bookable well in advance. On the fast inter-city services, you may have to reserve a seat, and will probably have to pay a supplement (**Zuschlag**). Many have first-class compartments only.

TEE	**Trans-Europ-Expreß**	1st class only, luxury, high-speed train
EC	**Eurocity** ⎫	V. fast, long-distance trains with restaurants, telephones, conference cars; supplement payable
IC	**Intercity** ⎬	
FD	**Fern-Expreß-Zug** ⎫	Fast trains, supplement for journeys under 50 km
D	**Schnellzug** ⎬	
E	**Eilzug** ⎭	Medium-distance train stopping at larger towns
N	**Nahverkehrszug**	Local stopping train
	Städteschnellzug	Fast inter-city train in Austria
	Schnellzug ⎫	Fast medium and long-distance trains in Austria and Switzerland
	Expreßzug ⎬	

Look out for these notices:

ABFAHRT	departures	**BESETZT**	engaged
ANKUNFT	arrivals	**FAHRKARTEN**	tickets
AUSKUNFT	information	**FAHRKARTEN-**	automatic ticket
GLEIS 3	platform (track) 3	**AUTOMAT**	machine
BAHNSTEIG 9	platform 9	**RAUCHER**	smoker
FREI	vacant	**NICHTRAUCHER**	non-smoker

the way it works

Verbs

vergessen *to forget*
ich **vergesse**   *I forget*   wir **vergessen**
du **vergißt**   Sie **vergessen**
Sie **vergessen**
er/sie/es **vergißt**   sie **vergessen**

sehen *to see*
ich **sehe**   *I see*   wir **sehen**
du **siehst**   Sie **sehen**
Sie **sehen**
er/sie/es **sieht**   sie **sehen**

Man

In German, **man** means 'one', 'people', 'you', 'they', etc.:

In London hat **man** auch Museen.   They have museums in London too.
Man kann zu Fuß in den Park gehen.   You can go to the park on foot.
Man kann das nicht sagen.   One can't say that.

Adjectives

When following **ein, mein** etc., adjectives take these endings:

masc.	*fem.*	*neuter*
ein herrlich**er** Park	eine alt**e** Kirche	ein interessant**es** Museum
mein jung**er** Mann	meine klein**e** Schwester	mein lieb**es** Kind

Welcher (which)

Welcher works like **dieser**:
welcher Zug (m)   which train
welches Boot (n)   which boat

welche Straße (f)   which street
welche Busse (pl.)   which buses

things to do

3.3   You want to go to Frankfurt. Ask the booking office clerk:
   1   When is the next train to Frankfurt?
   2   From which platform?
   3   Do you have to change?
       What time does it arrive? (**ankommen**)
   5   Can you book a seat?

CHANGING MONEY

Currency exchange Banking hours are 8.30–1.00 and 2.30–6.00 from Monday to Friday (5.30 on Thursdays or occasionally Fridays in large towns). Currency exchange bureaux (**Wechselstube**) at frontiers, stations, airports etc. are generally open outside banking hours, but will not give you such a good rate of exchange. Traveller's cheques and Eurocheques can be used in most hotels and shops in big cities, and the major credit cards are almost universally accepted.

In Germany, the currency is the **Deutsche Mark (DM)**, which is divided into 100 Pfennige (Pf.). In Austria, the currency is **Schillinge** (divided into 100 Groschen); in Switzerland, it is **Franken** (divided into 100 Rappen).

in der Bank/at the bank

Helen wants to buy some stamps for her postcards, but first Ulrike takes her to the bank to change some money.

Bankbeamter:	Guten Morgen. Was wünschen Sie, bitte?
Helen:	Guten Morgen. **Ich möchte einen Reisescheck einlösen.**
Bankbeamter:	Sehr gut. Ihren Paß, bitte.
Helen:	Sie brauchen meinen Paß? Er ist zu Hause!

Bankbeamter:	Es tut mir leid, aber ohne einen Paß können wir Reiseschecks nicht einlösen.
Helen:	Dann möchte ich **zwanzig Pfund in Deutsche Mark wechseln**.
Bankbeamter:	Wollen Sie bitte dieses Formular ausfüllen, und unterschreiben Sie hier. (While Helen is writing) So, Sie sind Engländerin.
Helen:	Ja, aus London. Bitte, **wie ist der Wechselkurs heute?**
Bankbeamter:	Er steht auf dem Anschlagbrett da drüben. Nehmen Sie dieses Papier und gehen Sie zur Kasse – dort wird man Ihnen das Geld geben

Geldwechseln (changing money)

die Bank/die Sparkasse	the bank/savings bank
der Bankbeamte	bank employee
Ich möchte einen Reisescheck einlösen	I'd like to cash a Traveller's cheque
Kann ich meine Euroschecks einlösen?	Can I cash my Eurocheques?
Ich möchte zwanzig Pfund in Deutsche Mark (um)wechseln/eintauschen	I'd like to change £20 into Marks
Wollen Sie bitte dieses Formular ausfüllen	Fill in this form please
Unterschreiben Sie hier	Sign here

Rates

Wie ist der Wechselkurs?	What is the exchange rate?
Er steht auf dem Anschlagbrett	It's on the noticeboard
Was macht das?	What does it come to?
Fünfundzwanzig Mark achtzig Pfennig	25 Marks and 80 Pfennigs
Nehmen Sie dieses Papier/diese Nummer	Take this paper/number
Gehen Sie zur Kasse	Go to the cash desk
Dort wird man Ihnen das Geld geben	They'll give you the money there

das Geld	money	**das Scheckbuch**	cheque book
das Bargeld	cash	**der Scheck**	cheque
das Kleingeld	change	**die Währung**	currency
der Geldschein/ die Banknote	(bank) note	**das Konto**	account
der 20-Mark-Schein	20 Mark note	**ein Konto eröffnen**	to open an account
der Kassen-schalter	cashier's window	**deponieren/ einzahlen**	to deposit
zahlen	to pay	**abheben**	to withdraw

Persönlicher Ausweis (personal identification)

Ihren Paß, bitte	Your passport, please
Ohne einen Paß können wir Reiseschecks nicht einlösen	We can't change traveller's cheques without a passport
Ich habe eine Scheckkarte	I have a cheque card
eine Kontokarte	a bank card
eine Kreditkarte	a credit card

USEFUL WORDS AND EXPRESSIONS

Er (der Paß) ist zu Hause! It's at home

Asking questions

Wer?	Who?	**Wie?**	How?	**Wann?**	When?
Was?	What?	**Wieviel?**	How much/many?	**Wo?**	Where?

Nationalities

Sprechen Sie langsam	Speak slowly
Ich spreche kaum Deutsch	I speak very little German
Ich spreche nur ein bißchen Deutsch	I only speak a little German
Ich habe kein Deutsch	I don't speak German
Ich verstehe Sie nicht	I don't understand you

Ich bin Engländerin	**Ich wohne in England**	**Ich spreche Englisch**
I am an Englishwoman	I live in England	I speak English
Ich bin Amerikaner	**Ich wohne in New York**	**Ich spreche Englisch**
I am an American	I live in New York	I speak English
deutsche Zeitungen	**australische Strände**	**schweizerische Küche**
German newspapers	Australian beaches	Swiss cooking

Countries and languages

die Bundesrepublik Deutschland	the Federal Republic of Germany
die Deutsche Demokratische Republik/ die DDR	the German Democratic Republic

Deutschland	**der Deutsche/die Deutsche**	**deutsch**
Germany	German (man/woman)	German (adj.)

the way it works

More prepositions

1   These prepositions are followed by nouns in the object case (i.e. **der** changes to **den** in the masculine singular): **bis** (until); **durch** (through); **für** (for); **gegen** (about, in return for, against); **ohne** (without); **um** (around, at).

2   You have seen how **der/die/das** change after the prepositions **mit, zu** and **in**. The following prepositions cause the same changes (i.e. **der** and **das** change to **dem**; **die** changes to **der**); **aus** (out of, from); **bei** (near, at the home of); **gegenüber*** (opposite); **nach** (after); **seit** (since).
*Note that with **gegenüber**, the noun comes before the preposition.

3   Some prepositions take either of the endings in (1) or (2) above, depending on whether there is any movement involved or implied (see p. 28). e.g.
Er **geht** hinter **das** Café (movt.)   Er **ist** hinter **dem** Café (no movt.)
an (at, to); **auf** (on); **hinter** (behind); **in** (in); **neben** (beside); **über** (over); **unter** (under); **vor** (in front of); **zwischen** (between).

4   *Contractions* Just as in + **das** can become **ins, von** + **dem** = **vom**, etc., other prepositions join with **der/die/das** to form contractions:

an + dem = **am**	an + das = **ans**
auf + das = **aufs**	bei + dem = **beim**
durch + das = **durchs**	für + das = **fürs**
hinter + das = **hinters**	über + das = **übers**

things to do

4.1   1   You see the notice 'Sparkasse'.
Is it **(a)** a bank   **(b)** an exchange bureau   **(c)** a cash desk?
2   You are looking for the exchange rate.
Is it **(a)** der Wechselkurs   **(b)** der Bankbeamte
(c) das Anschlagbrett?
3   The assistant says to you: 'Das macht fünfunddreißig Mark zehn Pfennig.'
Is it **(a)** DM25,10   **(b)** DM53,20   **(c)** DM35,10?
4   You want the assistant to give you some cash as well as notes. Do you ask for **(a)** der Geldschein   **(b)** das Geld   **(c)** das Bargeld?

4.2   You go into a bank to change some money. See if you can talk to the assistant in German:
1   Say you would like to change £50 into Marks.
2   Say you would like to cash a traveller's cheque.
3   Ask what the exchange rate is for today.
4   Ask if you can cash a Eurocheque. Say your passport is at the hotel, but you have a cheque card or (**oder**) a credit card.

BUYING STAMPS

Post Offices   Opening hours in Germany are 8.00–6.00 on Mondays to Fridays and 8.00–12.00 on Saturdays. In Austria they are 8.00–5.00 and in Switzerland 7.30–6.30 p.m., with a break for lunch at 12.00. Post offices at railway stations and in main cities are open until later in the evening on weekdays.

Letter boxes are yellow (sometimes blue in Austria). Stamps can be bought from the post office, from automatic machines outside post offices and telephone boxes, and from stationers' and newspaper stalls.

einen brief schicken/sending a letter

Postbeamter:	Bitte schön, meine Damen?
Helen:	**Wieviel kostet eine Postkarte nach England**, bitte?
Postbeamter:	Siebzig Pfennig.
Helen:	Und **was kostet ein Brief**?
Postbeamter:	Nach England? Das kostet neunzig Pfennig.
Helen:	Geben Sie mir bitte **fünf Briefmarken zu siebzig** und eine zu neunzig.
Postbeamter:	Fünf Stück zu siebzig und eine zu neunzig, das sind zusammen . . .
Helen:	Oh, und **ich muß auch eine Postkarte** in die Vereinigten Staaten **senden**.
Ulrike:	Und **ich möchte dieses Paket** nach Freiburg **schicken**.
Postbeamter:	Moment mal, meine Damen. Ich suche meinen Rechner!

Im Postamt (at the post office)

die Deutsche Bundespost	German Federal postal service
der Postbeamte	post office clerk
der Brief (pl. die Briefe)	letter
die Briefmarke/das Paket	stamp/parcel
Wieviel kostet eine Postkarte nach England, bitte?	How much is a postcard to England, please?
Was kostet ein Brief nach Italien?	How much is a letter to Italy?
Was kostet ein Paket nach Australien?	How much is a parcel to Australia?
Nach England? Das kostet neunzig Pfennig	For England? That's 90 Pfennigs
Geben Sie mir fünf Briefmarken zu siebzig und eine zu neunzig	Give me 5 stamps at 70 Pf. and one at 90 Pf.
Fünf Stück zu siebzig . . .	Five at 70 pf. . . .
Ich möchte eine Postkarte in die Vereinigten Staaten senden/schicken	I'd like to send a postcard to the USA
Ich möchte ein Paket nach Freiburg schicken	I'd like to send a parcel to Freiburg
per Luftpost/per Normaltarif	by air/by surface mail
per Einschreiben/per Expreß	registered/express mail
Was macht das?	How much is that?
Das sind zusammen . . .	Altogether that comes to . . .
Ich möchte eine Internationale Postanweisung einlösen	I'd like to cash an international money order
Ich möchte ein Telegramm aufgeben	I'd like to send a telegram
Wo ist der Briefkasten?	Where is the post box?
das Postfach	post office box
Moment mal, meine Damen. Ich suche meinen Rechner	Just a moment, ladies. I'm looking for my calculator

POST/POSTAMT	post office
POSTWERT-ZEICHEN BRIEFMARKEN	stamps
BRIEFMARKEN AUTOMAT	automatic stamp machine
POSTLAGERNDE SENDUNG	poste restante
PAKETE	parcels
TELEGRAMME	telegrams

the way it works

Indirect object pronouns

1   Pronouns too alter after prepositions. You have already seen how they change after **für, ohne**, etc. This is how they change after **mit, zu, von**, etc. These pronouns are said to be in the indirect object, or dative case:

mit mir	with me	**mit uns**	with us
zu dir	to you		
von Ihnen	from you	**von Ihnen**	from you (pl.)
bei ihm/ihr	near him/her	**bei ihnen**	near them

2   Indirect object pronouns occur after certain verbs. In many cases, these are the same in English, e.g. **geben** (to give):

	indirect object	*direct object*
ich gebe	**ihr**	das Formular
I give	(to) her	the form

You will find indirect object pronouns after these verbs: bringen (to bring), schicken (to send), danken (to thank), senden (to send), geben (to give), zeigen (to show), helfen (to help).

More verbs

wollen *to want*		**sprechen** *to speak*	
ich **will**	wir **wollen**	ich **spreche**	wir **sprechen**
du **willst**	Sie **wollen**	du **sprichst**	Sie **sprechen**
Sie **wollen**		Sie **sprechen**	
er/sie/es **will**	sie **wollen**	er/sie/es **spricht**	sie **sprechen**

werden *to become*	
ich **werde**	wir **werden**
du **wirst**	Sie **werden**
Sie **werden**	
er/sie/es **wird**	sie **werden**

In the future

When talking about something that is going to happen in the future, use **werden** plus a verb in the infinitive, e.g.

ich **werde fragen** (I will/shall ask)   wir **werden suchen** (we will look for)
du **wirst antworten** (you will answer)   Sie **werden geben** (you will give)
sie **wird kommen** (she will come)   sie **werden nehmen** (they will take)

His and her

In German, these are **sein** and **ihr**:

sein Bruder	his brother	**sein** Haus	his house
ihr Bruder	her brother	**ihr** Haus	her house
seine Tochter	his daughter	**seine** Kinder	his children
ihre Tochter	her daughter	**ihre** Kinder	her children

things to do

4.3   You are in a German post office.
  1   First you want to know if any post has arrived for you. What sign do you look for?
  2   You want to send a letter to England. What do you ask the counter clerk?
  3   You want to buy three stamps at 70 Pfennig. What do you say?
  4   Say you would like to send a parcel to New York, and ask how much it comes to.
  5   Say you would like to cash an international money order.
  6   Ask how much it costs to send a postcard to Australia.

HIRING A CAR

Motoring   Germany, Austria and Switzerland have many miles of
motorway (**Autobahn**) and good linking roads. Germany has 4,600 miles of
motorways without tolls, Austria has some toll motorways and in
Switzerland motorway users must obtain special windscreen stickers.
There are road patrols on motorways and major roads, and in Germany
motorway petrol stations and restaurants often display boards giving
useful information about the district.

When driving, seat-belts must be worn, and children under 12 must travel
in the back of the car. Third-party insurance is compulsory, but visitors
from EEC countries do not need Green Card insurance for driving in
Germany. Motorists must carry a red warning triangle and a first-aid kit,
and headlights must be dipped when driving in foggy conditions. Use
headlights or dipped headlights at dusk. On Alpine roads, snow tyres and
chains must be used in winter.

Car hire   There are car hire offices at over 40 main railway stations in
Germany. Cars can also be delivered to airports and hotels. Rates vary
from place to place, and you may be charged by the kilometre or by the
day. In larger towns, chauffeur-driven transport is also available. On the
continent, don't forget to drive on the right!

bei der Autovermietung/at the car hire office

On Friday, George Jackson has a free morning. He hires a car in order to take Helen, Gisela and Thomas into the countryside.

George: Guten Morgen. **Ich möchte ein Auto** mieten, bitte.

Angestellter: Sicherlich. Für vier Personen? Wir haben einen mittleren Volkswagen, oder einen großen Audi mit Automatik. Der Audi hat auch ein Radio mit Kassettenrecorder.

George: **Bezahlt man pro Tag oder pro Kilometer?**

Angestellter: Es kommt darauf an . . .

Thomas: Toll! Wieviel kostet der Audi?

Angestellter: (handing George a form) Hier sind die Gebühren und die Versicherungskosten. Aber, entschuldigen Sie bitte, ist das Auto für den Herrn, oder wird dieser junge Mann auch fahren?

George: (hastily) Nein, nein – nur ich. Also, **wir nehmen den VW**, danke.

Angestellter: Zeigen Sie mir bitte Ihren Führerschein. (He checks the document) Alles ist in Ordnung, Herr Jackson. Hier ist der Schlüssel. Kommen Sie mit mir, wir sehen das Auto an . . .

Hiring a car

die Autovermietung	car hire office
Ich möchte ein Auto/einen Wagen mieten	I'd like to hire a car
Für wie lange?	For how long?
Sicherlich. Für vier Personen?	Of course. For four?
Wir haben einen mittleren VW . . . einen großen Audi	We have a medium-sized VW . . . a large Audi
mit Automatik	automatic
Er hat ein Radio mit Kassettenrecorder	It has a radio with a cassette-player.
Bezahlt man pro Tag oder pro Kilometer?	Do you pay by the day or by the kilometre?
Wieviel kostet der Audi?	How much does the Audi cost?
Wieviel kostet es für einen Tag/eine Woche?	How much does it cost for a day/a week?
Hier sind die Gebühren und die Versicherungskosten	Here are the charges and the insurance costs
Muß ich eine Kautionssumme zahlen?	Do I have to pay a deposit?
Nein, wenn Sie mit einer Kreditkarte bezahlen, dann nicht	No, if you pay by credit card
Kann ich den Wagen in Frankfurt lassen?	Can I leave the car in Frankfurt?
Wir nehmen den VW, danke	We'll take the VW, thank you

Zeigen Sie mir Ihren Führerschein	Show me your driving licence
Alles ist in Ordnung	Everything is in order
Hier ist der Schlüssel	Here is the key
Wir sehen das Auto an	We'll have a look at the car
die Vollkaskoversicherung	full insurance cover
der Führerschein/die Autopapiere	driving licence/car documents
Gute Fahrt!	Have a good trip!

On the road (auf den Weg)

das Auto	car	das Moped	moped
der Lastkraft-	lorry	der Motorroller	scooter
wagen (LKW)		das Fahrrad	bicycle
der Wohnwagen	caravan	der Verkehr	traffic
der Reisebus	coach	die Verkehrstauung	traffic jam
das Motorrad	minibus	die Geschwindig-	speed limit
der Kleinbus	motorcycle	keitsbegrenzung	

DRIVING

▶ **Restrictions and breakdown** Speed limits are 50 km/hr (32 mph) in built-up areas and villages (60/38 in Switzerland), and 100 (62) on all other roads except motorways and dual-carriageways. On German motorways there are no limits, but 130 (82) is the recommended maximum speed. If you are stopped for breaking a limit, you will have to produce your licence and you may be fined on the spot. Breathalyser tests are in operation and drinking and driving is a serious offence. If you are over the limit you will lose your licence immediately.

Traffic signs are international. In town parking zones, discs (**Parkscheiben**) can be bought from petrol stations, tobacconists' and tourist offices.

Emergency telephones are situated on motorways, and in Germany, the ADAC (**Allgemeiner Deutscher Automobil Club**) runs an emergency breakdown service (**Straßenwachthilfe**). They also advise foreign motorists who are members of affiliated organisations, and publish maps and guidebooks.

At the filling station (an der Tankstelle)

die Tankstelle	filling station
Selbsttanken/Selbstbedienung	self-service
Ich brauche Benzin	I need some petrol
Super/Normal/Diesel/bleifreies Benzin	4-star/2-star/diesel/lead-free petrol
Fünfundzwanzig Liter Benzin, bitte	25 litres of petrol, please
Für zwanzig Mark Super	20 Marks' worth of 4-star
Volltanken, bitte	Fill it up, please
Normal voll, bitte	Fill it up with 2-star, please
Bitte prüfen Sie . . .	Please check . . .
das Öl/das Wasser/die Reifen/die Batterie	the oil/water/tyres/battery
den Reifendruck prüfen	check the tyre pressure
Führen Sie Reparaturen aus?	Do you do repairs?

In town

Darf ich hier parken?	Can I park here?
die Parkuhr	parking meter
der Parkplatz	car park
die Hochgarage	multi-storey park
die Parkscheibe	parking disc

eine Panne/a breakdown

George and the three young people stop at a village to admire the view, but unfortunately, the car seems to be giving some trouble.

Thomas: Was ist los, Herr Jackson? Brauchen wir vielleicht Benzin?

George: (Trying to start the car) Himmel, **der Wagen springt nicht an!** (He tries again) Nein, **da ist etwas kaputt!** Gisela, dort drüben steht eine Telefonzelle. Rufen Sie sofort eine Reparaturwerkstatt an.

am Apparat/on the phone

Gisela: Hallo? Führen Sie Reparaturen aus? **Ich möchte den Mechaniker sprechen**, bitte.

Angestellte: Einen Augenblick, bitte . . . Das tut mir leid, er ist gerade nicht da.

Gisela: **Würden Sie bitte etwas ausrichten?** Mein Name ist Fräulein Bauer, und mein VW hat im Dorf eine Panne. Bitte schicken Sie sobald wie möglich den Mechaniker.

Angestellte: Danke. **Auf Wiederhören.**

At the garage (in der Reparaturwekstatt)

die Reparaturwerkstatt	repairs garage
Ich habe einen Unfall gehabt	I've had an accident
Mein Auto hat eine Panne	My car has broken down
Es steht zwei Kilometer von hier	It's 2 km from here
Ich habe kein Benzin mehr im Tank	I've run out of petrol
Ich habe eine Reifenpanne	I've got a puncture
Können Sie den Reifendruck prüfen?	Can you check the tyre pressure?
Mein Wagen springt nicht an	My car won't start
Die Batterie ist leer	The battery is flat
Der Motor geht aus	The engine is stalling
Schicken Sie sobald wie möglich einen Mechaniker	Send a mechanic as soon as possible
der Abschleppwagen	breakdown lorry
der Anlasser/die Blinker	the starter/indicators
. . . ist/sind nicht in Ordnung	. . . isn't/aren't working
. . . funkioniert/funktionieren nicht	. . . isn't/aren't working
(For a list of car parts, see p. 80)	
Können Sie mir bitte einen Kostenvoranschlag geben?	Please can you give me an estimate?
Wann wird das Auto fertig sein?	When will the car be ready?

Road signs

AUTOBAHN	motorway	**HALT**	stop
AUSFAHRT	exit	**MAUTSTELLE**	toll (Austria)
EINFAHRT	entrance	**UMLEITUNG**	diversion
GEFAHR	danger	**VORSICHT**	careful
GRENZE	border		
GRENZ-KONTROLLE	border control		

Bauarbeiten	road works
Blaue Zone	restricted parking zone
Durchfahrt verboten	no through road
Einbahnstraße	one-way street
Einordnen	get in lane
Keine Einfahrt	no entry
Langsam fahren	drive slowly
Rechts fahren	keep to the right
Überholen verboten	no overtaking
Vorfahrt beachten	give way

Telephones   Calls can be made from the post office or public call boxes (**Fernsprecher**). Long-distance calls can be made from most call boxes in Germany and Switzerland, and from some in Austria. Look out for the signs **Ausland/International**. Instructions are often translated into English. To phone abroad, dial 00, then the country code followed by the town code minus the 0. For local calls, the dialling codes are given next to the place name in the directory. In Germany, the minimum charge for a call box is 20 Pf. (at least DM1,– for international calls). Phoning from hotels is far more expensive than using public phone boxes.

Using the telephone

das Telefon	telephone	die Vermittlung	operator
die Telefon- nummer	phone number	die Auskunft	enquiries
		ein Nummer wählen	dial a number
das Telefonbuch	directory		
die Telefonzelle	phone box	das Ortgespräch	local call
die Vorwähl- nummer	dialling code	das Ausland- gespräch	international call
das Amtszeichen	dialling tone		

telefonieren/anrufen	to telephone
Wo kann ich telefonieren?	Where can I make a phone call?
Dort drüben steht eine Telefonzelle	There's a phone box over there
Rufen Sie sofort eine Reparaturwerkstatt an	Phone a garage straight away
Ich brauche Münzen	I need some coins
Münzeinwurf/Münzrückgabe	Insert coins/Returned coins
Kann ich bitte ein Amt haben?	May I have a line please?
Hallo, hier Jackson	Hello, this is Mr Jackson
Jackson am Apparat	Mr Jackson speaking.
Ich möchte den Mechaniker sprechen	I'd like to speak to the mechanic
Ich hätte gern Apparat hundertzwo*	I'd like extension 102
ein Gespräch mit Voranmeldung	a person-to-person call
ein R-Gespräch	a reverse charge call
Wieviel kostet es?	How much does it cost?

48   *On the phone, use **zwo** not **zwei**

Understanding the reply

Wer ist am Apparat?	Who's speaking?
Einen Augenblick, bitte	Just a moment
Bitte warten Sie	Please wait
Ich verbinde Sie	I'm putting you through
Bleiben Sie am Apparat	Hold the line
Es ist besetzt	The line's engaged
Es antwortet niemand/keiner.	There's no answer
Sie haben sich verwählt	You've got the wrong number
Das tut mir leid, er ist gerade nicht da	I'm sorry, he's not there at the moment
Würden Sie bitte später nochmal versuchen?	Do you want to try again later?
Danke, ich rufe wieder an	Thanks, I'll ring back
Würden Sie bitte etwas ausrichten?	Please could you take a message?
Meine Telefonnummer ist . . .	My phone number is . . .
Ich komme nicht durch	I can't get through
Ich bin unterbrochen worden	I've been cut off
Auf Wiederhören!	Goodbye!

USEFUL WORDS AND EXPRESSIONS

Es kommt darauf an . . .	It depends . . .
Toll!	Fantastic!
Wird dieser junge Mann auch fahren?	Will this young man be driving too?
Nur ich	Just me
Himmel!	Heavens!

the way it works

Verbs which separate

Some verbs in German separate into two parts when not in the infinitive, and the first part normally goes to the end of the sentence. Here are some examples:

ansehen to look at   Wir **sehen** das Auto **an**. (We look at the car.)
anspringen to start (engine)   Der Wagen **springt** nicht **an**. (The car doesn't start.)
anrufen to call, phone   **Rufen** Sie eine Reparaturwerkstatt **an**. (Call a garage.)
zurückkommen to come back   Der Mechaniker **kommt** um 8 Uhr **zurück**. (The mechanic is coming back at 8 o'clock.)
ausführen to carry out   Er **führt** die Reparaturen **aus**. (He does the repairs.)

More about adjectives

You may have noticed that when **der/die/das** are not mentioned, adjectives take these endings:

schwarz**er** Kaffee (m)   weiß**e** Limonade (f)   stark**es** Bier (n)

Adjectives which come before the noun change in the object case as follows:

	masc.	fem.	neuter
Ich sehe	den groß**en** Audi	die kleine Tür	das alte Fahrrad
Wir haben	einen groß**en** Audi	eine kleine Tür	ein alte**s** Fahrrad

things to do

5.1 You are at a filling station in Germany.
1 Ask for 30 litres of 4-star petrol.
2 Ask if you can check the tyre pressure.
3 Ask if they can check the battery.
4 Ask whether they do repairs.

5.2 You are hiring a car.
1 Say you would like a small car.
2 Ask how much it costs for 2 days.
3 Ask if you have to pay a deposit.
4 Say you want to leave the car in Stuttgart.
5 Say you'll take the blue Volkswagen and ask for the key.

5.3 1 You are on the motorway and looking for the exit. What sign do you look for?
2 You see the sign **EINBAHNSTRAßE.** Does it mean **(a)** no through road **(b)** one-way street **(c)** pedestrians only?
3 You need to buy a parking disc. Is it **(a)** eine Parkuhr **(b)** eine Parkscheibe **(c)** einen Parkplatz?

5.4 **A** Helen answers the phone at the Bauer's house. What does she say?

Frau Schott: Hallo, bist du es, Ulrike?
Helen: [No, this is Helen Jackson.]
Frau Schott: Oh, entschuldigen Sie. Hier Frau Schott – darf ich Frau Bauer sprechen?
Helen: [Wait a moment . . . I'm sorry, she's not here.]
Frau Schott: Wann kommt sie wieder zurück?
Helen: [She's coming back at half past five, I think.]
Frau Schott: Danke, ich versuche später nochmal.
Helen: [Goodbye.]

B Now Helen tries to ring Thomas at his flat, but he doesn't seem to be there. Günther answers the phone.

Günther: Hallo, hier Günther Rascher.
Helen: [I'd like to speak to Thomas, please.]
Günther: Leider ist er gerade nicht da. Wer ist am Apparat, bitte?
Helen: [It's Helen Jackson speaking.]
Günther: Ach so. Wollen Sie eine Nachricht für ihn hinterlassen?
Helen: [No, I'll call back later.]
Günther: Gut. Auf Wiederhören.
Helen: [Goodbye.]

HEALTH PROBLEMS

Health   There is a reciprocal agreement between EEC countries for free
hospital and medical treatment, though prescription charges and
ambulances have to be paid for. Form E111 should be obtained from the
DHSS before setting out on your journey in order to claim reimbursement.
It is generally advisable, however, to take out private medical insurance
from a travel agent or motoring organisation, especially for winter sports
holidays.

Surgery hours are normally 10.00–12.00 and 4.00–6.00 (except weekends
and Wednesdays).

ein Unfall/an accident

Nach dem Mittagessen machen die jungen Leute einen kurzen
Spaziergang in das Dorf. George aber bleibt im Auto und hört Radio.
(*After lunch, the youngsters go for a short walk into the village. However,
George stays in the car and listens to the radio.*)

Helen:	Die Landschaft ist sehr schön – aber wo ist Thomas?
Eine Stimme:	Hilfe!
Gisela:	(running up) Thomas, was ist los?
Thomas:	**Ich bin hingefallen** . . .
Gisela:	Bist du verletzt? Wo hast du Schmerzen?

Thomas: **Ach, ich kann den Fuß nicht bewegen. Er tut mir weh! Mein Knöchel ist gebrochen,** glaube ich.

Helen: Ja, **der Fuß ist sehr geschwollen.** Guck mal die große blaue Quetschung!

Gisela: Er muß vielleicht ins Krankenhaus!

(Back at the car)

George: Lassen Sie mich sehen, junger Mann.

Thomas: Ah, vorsichtig!

George: So, das ist sicherlich eine Muskelzerrung. Gibt es eine Apotheke in diesem Dorf? Der Apotheker wird uns beraten.

Bei der Apotheke (At the chemist's)

Gisela: Er ist ein Unfall passiert. Mein Bruder hat große Schmerzen im Knöchel.

Apotheker: Wie fühlen Sie sich?

Thomas: **Schlecht. Mir ist schwindlig.**

Helen: Hat er Fieber?

Apotheker: Nein, die Temperatur is nicht hoch. Machen Sie sich keine Sorgen, das ist nichts Ernstes. Nehmen Sie dieses Schmerzmittel, und ruhen Sie sich aus.

Gisela: **Wieviel** soll er **einnehmen?**

Apotheker: **Zwei Tabletten, dreimal am Tag.**

Thomas: Nein, nein, keine Droge für mich. Heutzutage nehme ich nur homöopathische Mittel!

Seeking medical aid

(A list of parts of the body is given on p. 81)

Was ist los?	What's the matter?/What's up?
Ich bin hingefallen	I fell over
Bist du verletzt?	Are you hurt?
Ich habe Schmerzen	I'm in pain
Ich bin krank	I'm ill
der Arzt/das Krankenhaus	doctor/hospital
die Krankenschwester	nurse
die Röntgenaufnahme	X-ray
die Sprechstunden	surgery hours
Ich brauche einen Arzt	I need a doctor
Wo ist die nächste Arztpraxis?	Where is the nearest surgery?
Ich möchte einen Termin	I'd like an appointment
Ich bin angemeldet	I have an appointment
der ärztliche Notdienst	emergency service

Explaining what's wrong

Mein(e) . . . tut weh	My . . . hurts
Wo hast du Schmerzen?	Where does it hurt?
Ich kann den Fuß nicht bewegen	I can't move my foot
Mein Knöchel ist geschwollen/ gebrochen/verstaucht	My ankle is swollen/broken/sprained
Mein Bruder hat große Schmerzen im Knöchel	My brother has a bad pain in his ankle
Guck mal die große blaue Quetschung!	Look at the big blue bruise!
Vorsichtig!	Be careful!
Es tut mir weh	It hurts
Ich habe etwas im Auge	I've got something in my eye
Ich habe mir die Hand verbrannt	I've burned my hand
Ich bin gestochen/gebissen worden	I've been stung/bitten
Ich kann nicht schlafen/atmen	I can't sleep/breathe
Ich habe mich übergeben/ich habe erbrochen	I've been sick
Ich habe Magenschmerzen	I have stomach ache
Kopfschmerzen/Ohrenschmerzen	a headache/earache
Husten/Halsschmerzen	a cough/sore throat
Durchfall	diarrhoea
Ich bin Diabetiker/Asthmatiker	I'm diabetic/asthmatic
Ich bin herzkrank	I have heart trouble
Ich bin gegen Penizillin allergisch.	I'm allergic to penicillin
Ich bin schwanger	I'm pregnant
Ich nehme die Pille	I'm on the pill
Keine Droge für mich	No drugs for me
Heuzutage nehme ich nur homöopathische Mittel	These days I only take homeopathic remedies
Lassen Sie mich sehen	Let me see
Wie fühlen Sie sich?	How do you feel?
Schlecht. Mir ist schwindlig	Bad. I feel dizzy
Ich fühle mich nicht wohl	I don't feel well
Hat er Fieber?	Has he got a temperature?
Die Temperatur ist nicht hoch	His temperature isn't high
Das ist sicherlich eine Muskelzerrung	That's surely a torn muscle
Er muß vielleicht ins Krankenhaus	Perhaps he'll have to go to hospital
Sie müssen im Bett bleiben	You must stay in bed
Sie brauchen eine Spritze/einen Bluttest	You need an injection/a blood test
Machen Sie sich keine Sorgen	Don't worry.
Das ist nichts Ernstes	It's not serious.

Chemist Opening hours are 9.00–6.00 on Mondays to Fridays and until 2.00 on Saturdays. An **Apotheke** (recognisable by the sign of a red A) is a dispensing chemist's, whereas a **Drogerie** is similar to a drugstore, selling cosmetics, films etc. as well as some medicines. The chemist will give you helpful medical advice, first aid treatment, or refer you to a doctor if necessary. Details of chemists' rotas for nights (**NACHTSDIENST**) and Sundays (**SONNTAGSDIENST**) are posted up on the door of the shop.

At the chemist's (bei der Apotheke)

(For a list of items at the chemist's, see p. 78)

die Apotheke	dispensing chemist/pharmacy
dienstbereite Apotheken	chemists on rota
die Drogerie	chemist's shop/drugstore
Wo ist die nächste Apotheke?	Where is the nearest chemist's?
Gibt es eine Apotheke in diesem Dorf?	Is there a chemist's in this village?
Der Apotheker wird uns beraten	The chemist will advise us
Geben Sie mir bitte . . .	Please can I have . . .

Minor problems

Ich habe Insektenstiche/Heufieber Reisekrankheit/Sonnenbrand	I have insect bites/hay fever travel sickness/sunburn
Ich nehme dieses Medikament	I take this medicine
Ich brauche etwas/Tabletten gegen . . .	I need something/tablets for . . .
Ich habe ein Rezept	I have a prescription
Nehmen Sie dieses Schmerzmittel	Take this painkiller
Wieviel soll ich einnehmen?	How many should I take?
Zwei Tabletten, dreimal am Tag	Two tablets three times a day
einmal, zweimal	once, twice
alle vier Stunden/täglich/stündlich	every four hours/daily/hourly
vor/nach dem Essen	before/after meals
Keine Droge für mich	No drugs for me
Ruhen Sie sich aus	Rest yourself

At the dentist's (bei dem Zahnarzt)

der Zahnarzt	dentist
Ich habe Zahnschmerzen wundes Zahnfleisch	I've got toothache sore gums
Ich habe eine Füllung verloren	I've lost a filling
Dieser Zahn ist abgebrochen	This tooth is broken

OTHER EMERGENCIES

Problems If disaster strikes, go to the police station (**Polizeiwache**), the embassy, or ask for help at the hotel. *Wichtige Rufnummer* (important numbers): for the police, dial 110 (Germany); 133 (Austria); 117 (Switzerland).

Disasters

Hilfe!	Help!	Gefahr!	Danger!
Polizei!	Police!	Feuer!	Fire!
Notausgang	Emergency Exit	Vorsicht	Caution
Bergwacht	Mountain rescue	Schwimmweste	Lifejacket
Rettungsdienst	First aid/ ambulance	Rettungsgürtel	Lifebelt
		Feuerlöscher	Fire-extinguisher

Holen Sie Hilfe!	Fetch help!
Wo ist die Polizeiwache?	Where is the police station?
das Krankenhaus?	hospital?
Es ist ein Unfall passiert	There's been an accident
Rufen Sie bitte die Polizei	Call the police
die Feuerwehr/einen Arzt	the fire brigade/a doctor
einen Krankenwagen	an ambulance
Erste Hilfe	First aid

Der Autounfall (car accident)

Ich habe Vorfahrt gehabt	I had right of way
Es war Ihre Schuld	It was your fault
die Versicherungsgesellschaft	insurance company
einen Unfall melden	to report an accident
der Verletzte/die Geldstrafe	casualty/fine
die Blutprobe	blood test (for alcohol)

Loss and theft

Ich habe meinen Schlüssel verloren	I've lost my key
meinen Paß/meinen Fotoapparat	my passport/my camera
meine Scheckkarte/meine Karte	my cheque card/my ticket
Man hat meine Handtasche gestohlen	Someone's stolen my handbag
mein Portemonnaie/meine Brieftasche	my purse/my wallet
Ich habe mich verirrt	I'm lost
das Konsulat/die Botschaft	consulate/embassy
das Fundamt	lost property

USEFUL WORDS AND EXPRESSIONS

Die Landschaft ist sehr schön	The countryside is very pretty

55

the way it works

Expressions with mir and Ihnen

In German, it is common to us **mir** (to me) when talking about how you're feeling:

Wie geht es **Ihnen**?	How are you?
Mir ist schlecht.	I don't feel well.
Mir ist schwindlig.	I feel dizzy.
Mir is kalt.	I feel cold.

Notice also these expressions:

Es tut mir weh!	It hurts!
Es tut mir leid	I'm sorry
Wie gefällt es Ihnen?	How do you like it?
Mir ist das gleich/egal	It's all the same to me

Something good, nothing serious . . .

In these expressions, the words for 'good', 'serious' etc. take a capital letter and the ending **-es**:

etwas Gut**es**	something good	etwas Interessant**es**	something interesting
nichts Ernst**es**	nothing serious	nichts Neu**es**	nothing new

Reflexive pronouns

Wie fühlen Sie **sich**?	How are you feeling?
Ich ruhe **mich** aus.	I'm resting.

The **sich** and **mich** in these sentences correspond roughly to 'yourself', 'myself', and are known as reflexive pronouns, as they reflect the actions of the speaker. Many verbs can be reflexive or non-reflexive, e.g.:

Ich wasche den Audi	I wash the Audi.	(non-reflexive)
Ich wasche **mich**.	I wash myself, I get washed.	(reflexive)

Here is the full list of reflexive pronouns:

sich entschuldigen   *to excuse oneself*

ich **entschuldige mich** (*I excuse myself*)	wir **entschuldigen uns**
du **entschuldigst dich**	Sie **entschuldigen sich**
er/sie/es **entschuldigt sich**	sie **entschuldigen sich**

Some more verbs

tun *to do*		**dürfen** *to be allowed, (may)*	
ich **tue** (*I do*)	wir **tun**	ich **darf** (*I may*)	wir **dürfen**
du **tust**	Sie **tun**	du **darfst**	Sie **dürfen**
er/sie/es **tut**	sie **tun**	er/sie/es **darf**	sie **dürfen**

sollen *shall, ought to, should*		
ich **soll** (*I shall*)		wir **sollen**
du **sollst**		Sie **sollen**
er/sie/es **soll**		sie **sollen**

Like **können** and **müssen**, **dürfen** and **sollen** are so-called *modal verbs*, and are used very frequently in German, followed by the infinitive. Examples: Darf man hier rauchen?; Was soll ich tun?

things to do

5.5 Wo haben sie Schmerzen?

5.6 1 Your knee is sprained. Is it
(a) verstaucht (b) verbrannt (c) gebrochen?
2 You feel unwell and decide to consult the chemist.
(a) Ask where the nearest chemist's is.
(b) Say you have been sick, and ask if the chemist has something for stomachache.
(c) Say you have burnt your finger and you would like some pain-killers. Ask if you need a prescription.
(d) Ask how often (**wie oft**) you should take the tablets.
(e) Say you would also like some antiseptic and some cotton wool.

5.7 **Im Notfall . . .** (In an emergency . . .)
1 You have lost your traveller's cheques. What do you say?
(a) Ich habe meine Reiseschecks verloren.
(b) Ich habe meine Kreditkarten verloren.
(c) Ich habe meine Scheckkarten verloren.
2 Your luggage has been stolen. What do you tell the police?
(a) Man hat meinen Rucksack gestohlen.
(b) Man hat meine Reisetasche gestohlen.
(c) Man hat mein Gepäck gestohlen.
3 You have left your tickets at the hotel. How do you explain?
(a) Ich habe meine Tabletten im Hotel gelassen.
(b) Ich habe meine Karten im Hotel gelassen.
(c) Ich habe meine Brille im Hotel gelassen.

5.8 *Sie und Ihre Gesundheit* (You and your health)
Read this advertisement for an item which can be obtained from the chemist's. Can you say what it is?

> Schlafen Sie gut! *Ruhnox* ist das Naturrezept gegen Schlaflosigkeit. Ein Mittel, so alt wie die Menschheit, frisch aus der Natur, *Ruhnox* beruhigt die Nerven und fördert einen guten Schlaf, ohne jede Chemie. Hilft auch bei Nervosität und innerer Unruhe. Packung mit 50 Dragees, in Apotheken und Drogerien.

so alt wie	as old as	**jede**	every, all
die Menschheit	mankind	**die Unruhe**	restlessness

LEISURE AND SPORTS

▶ ▶ ▶ **Sport**   Sport is very popular, and all large towns have stadiums, swimming pools, etc. Horse-racing and riding are enjoyed in Germany, along with golf, tennis and fishing in the inland waterways. Football is extremely popular in Germany, Austria and Switzerland. Cycling is becoming increasingly popular, and in Germany bicycles can be hired at over 200 stations in touring areas. The skiing season runs from November to April and attracts visitors from all over the world. Skating and ice-hockey are also favourite winter pastimes.

im Sportzentrum/at the sports centre

It is late Saturday morning, and Helen goes with Gisela, Thomas and Karl-Heinrich to visit the sports centre.

Gisela: (proudly) Man kann hier im Sportzentrum an vielen verschiedenen Sportarten teilnehmen – es gibt Basketball, Handball, Schwimmen in der Schwimmhalle . . . normalerweise spielt der Thomas samstags Fußball, aber weil er verletzt ist, muß er heute Zuschauer sein, der Arme! Der Karl-Heinrich nimmt auch jede Woche Unterricht im Tennis. Wir haben hier herrliche Tennisplätze.

Thomas:	Tennis ist ein blöder Sport . . .
Gisela:	(continuing) Es gibt ein Radsport-stadion und eine Eissporthalle. Der Wintersport ist in Deutschland sehr populär.
Helen:	**Ich möchte gern Schlittschuhlaufen**, Gisela. **Kann man hier Schlittschuhe leihen?**
Gisela:	Ja, ja . . . Skier, Skistöcke, alles, was man für den Wintersport braucht.
Thomas:	Heute mittag findet ein Fußballspiel im Stadion statt. **Ich möchte das Spiel gern sehen!**
Gisela:	Toll – wir treffen uns um sechzehn Uhr zu Hause wieder. Aber Karl-Heinrich, du siehst sehr ärgerlich aus. Was ist denn los?
Karl-H.:	Du weißt, daß ich nicht gern Tennis spiele. **Ich will** auch **zum Fußball gehen** . . .

Im Sportzentrum (at the sport centre)

(For a list of sports, see p.80)

Ich treibe gern Sport	I like (I'm keen on) sport
Ich spiele gern Fußball	I like playing football
Mir gefällt das Schwimmen	I like swimming
Man kann an vielen verschiedenen Sportarten teilnehmen	One can take part in many different sporting activities
Es gibt viele Gelegenheiten	There are many facilities
Es gibt Basketball, Handball...	There's basketball, handball...
Schwimmen in der Schwimmhalle	swimming in the swimming hall
Est gibt ein Radsport-stadion und eine Eissporthalle	There's a cycle stadium and an ice stadium
normalerweise spielt der Thomas Fußball	Thomas normally plays football
weil er verletzt ist	since he's injured
muß er Zuschauer sein, der Arme!	he'll have to be a spectator, the poor thing!
Heute mittag findet ein Spiel im Stadion statt	There's a match taking place at midday in the stadium
Ich möchte gern das Spiel sehen	I'd love to see the match
Ich will zum Fußball gehen	I want to go to the football match
Karl-Heinrich nimmt Unterricht im Tennis	Karl-Heinrich is having tennis lessons
Wir haben herrliche Tennisplätze	We have lovely tennis courts

Tennis ist ein blöder/herrlicher/ gesunder Sport	Tennis is a stupid/fine/healthy sport
Du weißt, das ich nicht gern Tennis spiele	You know I don't like playing tennis
Der Wintersport ist sehr populär	Winter sports are very popular
Ich möchte gern Schlittschuhlaufen	I'd love to go skating
Kan man Schlittschuhe leihen?	Can one hire skates?
Wievel kostet es pro Stunde/ pro Tag?	How much does it cost per hour/ per day
Ich brauche Skier/Skistöcke	I need skis/ski sticks
alles, was man für den Wintersport braucht!	All you need for the winter sports!

USEFUL WORDS AND EXPRESSIONS

jede Woche	every week
wir treffen uns zu Hause wieder	we'll meet again at home
du siehst sehr ärgerlich aus	you look very cross
Was ist denn los?	What's up, then?

the way it works

Word order in more complicated sentences

Sometimes a sentence is made up of more than one clause. If the clauses are joined together by **und** (and) or **aber** (but), then both are main clauses and the word order is not affected:

Thomas ist verletzt, **und** er muß Zuschauer sein.
Karl-Heinrich nimmt Unterricht im Tennis, **aber** er will zum Fußball.

In many sentences however, there is one main clause and one or more secondary (subordinate) clauses. In subordinate clauses, the word order is changed and the verb goes to the end of the clause:

Thomas muß Zuschauer sein, **weil** er verletzt **ist.**
Gisela fragt den Karl-Heinrich, **warum** er ärgerlich **ist.**

As the main verb must always be the second idea in any sentence, note the word order when a subordinate clause comes first:

Weil er verletzt **ist**, **muß** Thomas Zuschauer **sein.**

Listen out for these words which will often introduce a subordinate clause:

als	when (in the past)	**warum**	why
weil	because, since	**wann**	when
da	since	**wie**	how, as
wenn	when, whenever, if	**wo**	where
ob	whether	**was**	that, which
daß	that		

Clauses are always separated by a comma in German:
Alles, was man für den Wintersport braucht.
Du weißt, daß ich nicht gern Tennis spiele.

To know

Wissen means 'to know' and is used for knowing facts, abstract ideas, etc.:
Du weißt, daß ich samstags Fußball spiele.
You know (that) I play football on Saturdays.
Wissen Sie, wo mein Schläger ist?
Do you know where my racquet is?

Here is the verb in full:

ich **weiß**	I know	wir **wissen**	we know
du **weißt**	you know	Sie **wissen**	you know
er/sie/es **weiß**	he/she/it knows	sie **wissen**	they know

things to do

6.1 Match up the items in the two columns to make sentences:

1	Im Freibad	**(a)**	findet ein Fußballspiel statt.
2	Auf der Eisbahn	**(b)**	gibt es einen Sessellift.
3	Im Stadion	**(c)**	kann man baden gehen.
4	Auf den Skigeländen	**(d)**	sieht man Fahrräder.
5	Im Radsport-stadion	**(e)**	spielt man Golf.
6	Am Golfplatz	**(f)**	geht man Schlittschuhlaufen.

6.2 **1** You need to hire some hiking equipment. Do you ask for:

(a) die Schneebrille
(b) den Taucheranzug
(c) die Wanderausrüstung?

2 You need skis, ski boots, ski sticks and a lift pass. Which can you *not* get from this shop?

Hier bekommen Sie Ihre
✷SKIER
SKISTIEFEL✷
✷LIFTPÄSSE

6.3

CLUB D-SPORT *Wenn Sie sich körperlich fit halten wollen!*	
Eintrittspreise	
(Erwachsene über 18 Jahre)	
Hallenbad (4 Stunden)	16,- DM
Schwimmbad mit Sauna (ganztägig)	19,- DM
Trainings-Raum	9,50 DM
Teilmassage	15,- DM
Solarium 10 Minuten	2,- DM
Bringen Sie Ihre Familie, Freunde und Bekannten mit!	

ganztägig all day **Bekannte** acquaintance

1 According to the tariff, how much do you pay for the swimming session only?
2 What can you have for 2 Marks?
3 Who do the advertisers suggest you bring with you?

ENTERTAINMENTS

What's on   There are theatres, cinemas and concert halls in all large towns. Many also have opera houses, some of which are world famous. You will find night clubs, discothèques, cafes and bars with live music (and **Bierkellers** in the south). In Hamburg and West Berlin, there is virtually non-stop entertainment.

You are expected to dress fairly formally for the theatre, opera, casinos and some restaurants. In the theatre, coats, umbrellas etc. should be deposited in the cloakroom (**Garderobe**), and the attendant will expect a small tip. There is generally no smoking in theatres and cinemas. Cinemas usually have separate performances and tickets can be reserved in advance. It is not necessary to tip cinema usherettes.

Museums are normally open from 9.00 to 5.00. Most close on Mondays (a few close on Saturdays or Sundays).

wohin heute abend?/where shall we go tonight?

It is early evening, and the Bauer family are planning an outing.

Gisela: Was gibt's heute abend zu tun?
Ulrike: Vielleicht gibt es ein neues Stück im Theater?

Thomas: **Ich möchte gern einen Film sehen.** Im Kino 'Royal' am Karslplatz läuft ein französischer Film mit Untertiteln.

Helen: **Was für ein Film ist das**, eine Komödie?

Thomas: Ich glaube schon – oder ein Krimi.

Ulrike: **Ich höre lieber ein gutes Konzert.** Hören Sie gern Musik, Helen? (looking at the paper) Im Staatstheater spielt man eine Mozart-Oper. Das wäre sehr schön!

Gisela: Mir ist Oper zu langweilig. (looks at her watch) **Um wieviel Uhr beginnt der Film?**

Thomas: Die Spätvorstellung fängt um zehn Uhr an und ist um halb eins zu Ende. Im 'Royal' kann man Plätze reservieren.

Gisela: Prima! **Gehen wir erst in eine Diskothek.** Ich will heute abend tanzen gehen!

in einem bayerischen Bierkeller/in a Bavarian ale-house

George and Ernst call in at "Zum Fässchen" for a drink after a hard day's work at the trade fair.

George: Es ist sehr gemütlich hier.

Ernst: Ja, und **samstags abends spielt man Jazz.** Interessieren Sie sich für Musik, George?

George: Ja, besonders für Jazz. Kennen Sie den berühmten amerikanischen Saxophonisten? . . . ich habe den Namen vergessen. Wir haben ihn letztes Jahr in London gehört. Es war wirklich wunderbar.

Ernst: Ich habe großen Durst. Was trinken Sie gern?

George: In einem Münchner Bierkeller trinkt man natürlich gutes Münchner Bier!

Was gibt's heute zu tun? (What is there to do today?)

die Veranstaltungen	events
(For a list of entertainments, see p. 81)	
Ich möchte zum Kino gehen	I'd like to go to the cinema
Ich habe Lust, einen Film zu sehen	I'd like to see a film
Ich möchte ein Konzert hören	I'd like to go to a concert
Ich würde gern das Museum besuchen	I'd like to visit the museum
Wann wird die Kunstgalerie geöffnet?	When does the gallery open?
Wann schließt das Museum?	When does the museum close?
Wieviel kostet die Eintrittskarte?	How much is the entrance?

ÖFFNUNGSZEITEN	opening hours	**EINTRITT FREI**	entrance free
GEÖFFNET	open	**GESCHLOSSEN**	closed
RUHETAG	closing day	**FOTOGRAFIEREN VERBOTEN**	no photographs

Cinema and theatre

Was gibt es heute im Kino zu sehen?/ Was läuft heute im Kino?	What's on at the cinema today?
Vielleicht gibt es ein neues Stück im Theater	Perhaps there's a new play on at the theatre
Im Kino läuft ein französischer Film mit Untertiteln/synchronisiert	There's a French film on at the cinema with sub-titles/dubbed
Was für ein Film/Stück ist das?	What kind of film/play is it?
eine Komödie/ein Trauerspiel/ein Krimi	a comedy/a tragedy/a thriller
ein Wildwestfilm/ein Zeichentrickfilm	a Western/a cartoon
das neues Stück/der neue Film von . . . wird im Theater gespielt/läuft im Kino	. . .'s new play/film is on at the theatre/cinema

Concert, opera, ballet

Ich höre lieber ein gutes Konzert	I'd rather go to a good concert
Hören Sie gern Musik?	Do you like listening to music?
Interessieren Sie sich für Musik?	Are you interested in music?
Im Staatstheater spielt man eine Mozart-Oper	There's a Mozart opera on at the State Theatre
Mir ist Oper zu langweilig	I find opera too boring
samstags spielt man Jazz	on Saturdays they have jazz
Kennen Sie den berühmten amerikanischen Saxophonisten?	Do you know the famous American saxophonist?
Wir haben ihn in London gehört	We heard him in London
es war wirklich wunderbar	it was really wonderful
Ich will tanzen gehen	I want to go dancing

Making booking enquiries

Um wieviel Uhr beginnt die Vorstellung?	What time does the performance begin?
Sie fängt um 10 Uhr an	It starts at 10 o'clock
die Theateraufführung	theatrical performance
die Nachmittagsvorstellung	matinée
die Spätvorstellung	late-night showing
durchgehende Vorstellung	continuous performance
Wie lange dauert es?	How long does it last?
Um wieviel Uhr ist der Film zu Ende?	What time does the film end?
Die Vorstellung endet um viertel vor neun	The performance ends at a quarter to nine
Wieviel kostet der Eintritt?	How much are the tickets?
Wie teuer?	What price range?
Kann ich Plätze reservieren?	Can I reserve the seats?
Es tut mir leid, es gibt keine Plätze mehr	I'm sorry, there aren't any seats left
Gibt es eine Ermäßigung für . . .	Is there a reduction for . . .
Kinder/Studenten/Gruppen	children/students/groups
Rentner/Behinderte/Arbeitslose?	pensioners/disabled/unemployed?

Buying a ticket

die Vorverkaufsstelle	booking office
Zweimal Parkett, bitte	Two in the stalls, please
Drei Plätze im ersten/zweiten Rang	Three seats in the dress/upper circle
Einen Platz im Balkon	One ticket in the circle
nach vorn/nach hinten	at the front/at the back

Likes and dislikes

Es gefällt mir	I like it
Es gefällt mir nicht	I don't like it
Die Musik gefällt mir	I like music
Ich finde das interessant/langweilig	I find it interesting/boring
Ich habe deutsche Filme gern	I like German films
Ich habe russisches Ballett nicht gern	I don't like the Russian ballet
Ich kann Oper nicht leiden	I hate opera
Ich kann Jazz nicht ausstehen	I loathe jazz

USEFUL WORDS AND EXPRESSIONS

ich glaube schon	I think so
Das wäre schön!	That would be lovely!
Prima!	Great!
es ist sehr gemütlich hier	it's very nice here
besonders	especially
ich habe den Namen vergessen	I've forgotten the (his) name
in einem Münchner Bierkeller	in a Munich ale-house

the way it works

Verbs with vowel changes

These verbs used in the dialogue have vowel changes for the parts that go with **er, sie** and **es**:

laufen: Im Kino **läuft** ein französischer Film   There's a French film on . . .
anfangen: Er **fängt** um 8 Uhr an   It starts at 8 o'clock

Other verbs with a similar vowel change are:
waschen (to wash): sie **wäscht**   fallen (to fall) es **fällt**

Word order

In a German sentence, use this order of words or phrases: **wann, wie, wo** (when, how, where):
Wir gehen **um elf Uhr zu Fuß ins Hotel zurück**.
We're going back to the hotel on foot at 11 o'clock.

Recognising the past tense

You may have noticed in *Freitag* some examples of verbs used in the past tense:
Ich **habe** meine Karten **verloren**   I have lost my tickets
Man **hat** meine Brieftasche gestohlen   Someone has stolen my wallet
You will see from these that **haben** is used together with a part of the verb known as
a **past participle**, which goes to the end of the sentence.

Many verbs form their past participles by adding **ge-** to the infinitive and
substituting -t for the -**en** ending, e.g.
machen: ich habe **ge**mach**t** (I made, I have made)
sagen: ich habe **ge**sagt (I said . . .)
hören: ich habe **ge**hör**t** (I heard . . .)
Some verbs do not appear to change, e.g.
vergessen: ich habe **vergessen** (I forgot, I have forgotten)
bekommen: ich habe **bekommen** (I got, I have got)
Many verbs change quite radically, e.g.
bringen (bring): ich habe **gebracht**   helfen (help): ich habe **geholfen**
denken (think): ich habe **gedacht**   verstehen (understand): **verstanden**
With some verbs, especially verbs of motion, **sein** is used instead of **haben** to make
the past tense:
kommen: ich **bin gekommen** (I came)   fahren: er **ist gefahren** (he drove)
gehen: Sie **sind gegangen** (you went)   bleiben: du **bist geblieben** (you stayed)
Listen out for **ich hatte** (I had), **ich war** (I was).

To know

Kennen also means 'to know', but is used for knowing people and places:
Kennen Sie den amerikanischen   Do you know the American
   Saxophonist**en**?*   saxophonist?
Kennen Sie meine Eltern?   Do you know my parents?
Ich kenne München sehr gut!   I know Munich very well!
*Some masculine nouns add an **n** or **en** in the object case.

things to do

6.4

NEUERÖFFNUNGEN: *Zum Schwarzen Storch* die Discothek für jedermann! ★		**Täglich geöffnet** ☆ **Im Herzen der Stadt** ☆ **Ab 20.00 Uhr** **Goethestr. gegenüber** **Hotel 'Münchner Hof'**

1 When was this discothèque opened?
2 Where is it situated?

3 When and at what time is it open?

6.5

Was möchten sie heute tun?
Can you say what each of these people wants to do today? e.g.
1 Er hat Lust, zum Theater zu gehen.

6.6

A
> ***GROSSER SAAL***   *19.30 Uhr   Samstag 3. Oktober*
> *Radio-Sinfonie-Orchester Frankfurt   Dirigent: Eliahu Inbal*
> *Großes Operettenkonzert mit Musik von Lehar, Offenbach und Strauß*
> *Balkon DM 20,-   Parkett DM 40,-*

B
> ***DEUTSCHES KUNSTINSTITUT***
> *Städtische Galerie*
> *Eintrittspreis: 3,00 DM*
> *öffnungszeiten: Dienstag bis Sonntag von 11.00 bis 18.00 Uhr*

C
> *Das Deutsche Künstlerische Kino präsentiert:*
> *neue Kürz-Filme aus Westdeutschland*
> *seit 6. Juni*

A You want to book for this concert.
1 Ask what time it ends.
2 Ask if there are reductions for students.
3 Say you'd like 2 tickets in the circle, at the front.

B A German colleague phones to ask about the art gallery, of which you have details.
1 Tell him how much it costs to get in.
2 Tell him what the opening hours are.
3 Tell him on which day it shuts.

C You are interested in the films advertised.
1 Ask what time the performance begins.
2 Ask if you can book seats.
3 Ask for a ticket in the stalls.

CAMPING AND HOLIDAYS

Camping   Camping is very popular and is highly organised, especially in Germany, where youth-hostelling and hiking are also favourite activities. There are hundreds of official camp-sites, many in picturesque areas – in the mountains or at the lakeside (details from the National Tourist Offices, the motoring organisations and the various published handbooks). It is also possible to camp in the countryside, providing you first obtain permission from the farmer and local police. The season is from May to September, but there are also a large number of winter camp-sites, especially in winter sports areas. Sites are not generally bookable in advance. Rates vary from place to place, but you can expect to pay per car, per person and per tent or caravan as well as for electricity and hot showers. In Germany, youth hostels are normally open to card-holders of all ages.

auf dem Campingplatz/at the camp-site

Gisela, Thomas and Günther are taking Helen camping in the countryside south of Munich on her last day in Germany.

Thomas:	Zelten wir hier unter den zwei großen Bäumen. Gisela, gib mir den Holzhammer und die Heringe fürs Zelt herüber, bitte.
Gisela:	(dreamily) Es ist so schön mitten im bayerischen Wald. Endlich kann man die frische Luft atmen – **und was für ein herrlicher Tag!** Es sind keine Wolken am Himmel. Sag mal, Thomas, **hast du die Wettervorhersage heute morgen gehört?**
Thomas:	Nein, aber es steht in der Zeitung, daß es dan ganzen Tag sonnig wird.
Günther:	(gloomily) Heute nacht wird es sicherlich kalt. Auf dem Boden onhe Zeltbetten erfriert man.

Thomas:	**Wir können hier im kleinen Campingladen Luftmatratzen mieten.**
Gisela:	Ja, und wir brauchen auch eine Landkarte mit Wanderwegen.
Günther:	(brightening): Komm, Helen, schauen wir uns den See an. Hast du deinen Badeanzug mitgebracht?
Thomas:	(rather put out) Erst steigen wir den Hügel hinauf. Von oben hat man eine großartige Aussicht, und man kann die fernen Berge mit ihren schneebedeckten Gipfeln noch sehen.
Gisela:	Ja, ja, und das kleine Kloster da unten . . .
Thomas:	Und das Schloß, das Ludwig II gebaut hat . . .
Helen:	(laughing) Moment mal – ich muß eine Kassette in meinen Fotoapparat einlegen!

Going camping

Zelten wir hier unter den zwei großen Bäumen	Let's camp here under the 2 tall trees
Gib mir den Holzhammer und die Heringe fürs Zelt (herüber)	Pass me the mallet and the tent pegs
mitten im Wald	in the middle of the wood
Auf dem Boden ohne Zeltbetten erfriert man	We'll freeze to death on the ground without camp beds
Wir können Luftmatratzen mieten	We can hire airbeds
im kleinen Campingladen	in the little camp-shop
eine Landkarte mit Wanderwegen	a map with footpaths
Darf man hier campen?	Can we camp here?
campen/zelten	camp/camp (pitch a tent)
Es kostet 6,– DM pro Nacht	It costs 6 marks a night

der Zeltplatz	pitch/site
das Zelt	tent
der Hering	peg
die Zeltstange	tent pole
der Schlafsack	sleeping bag
der Kocher	stove
das Camping-Gas	camping gas
die Taschenlampe	torch
der Waschraum	wash-room
der Laden	shop
der Stromanschluß	electricity
Streichhölzer	matches
der Korkenzieher	corkscrew

die Büchse	can
der Dosenöffner	can-opener
das Taschenmesser	penknife
die Wasserflasche	water bottle
der Wasserhahn	tap
Ist das Trinkwasser?	Is it drinking water?
der Wohnwagen	caravan
der Anhänger	trailer
die Jugendherberge	youth hostel

ZELTEN/CAMPING VERBOTEN　　　　*NO CAMPING*
KEIN TRINKWASSER　　　　　　　　*NOT DRINKING WATER*
TOILETTEN U. DUSCHEN　　　　　　*TOILETS & SHOWERS*

On holiday (in den Ferien)

Es steht in der Zeitung	It says in the paper
Man kann die frische Luft atmen	One can breathe the fresh air
Schauen wir uns den See an	Let's have a look at the lake
Steigen wir den Hügel hinauf	Let's climb up the hill
eine großartige Aussicht	a magnificent view
die fernen Berge	the distant mountains
mit ihren schneebedeckten Gipfeln	with their snowy peaks
das kleine Kloster da unten	the little monastery below
das Schloß, das der König gebaut hat	the castle that the king built

Talking about the weather

(For a list of weather vocabulary, see p. 80)

Was für ein herrlicher Tag!	What a glorious day!
Was für ein schrecklicher Tag!	What a dreadful day!
Was für ein schönes Wetter!	What lovely weather!
Was für ein furchtbares Wetter!	What terrible weather!
Hast du die Wettervorhersage gehört?	Have you heard the weather forecast?
Wie ist das Wetter?	What's the weather like?
Es sind keine Wolken am Himmel	There isn't a cloud in the sky
Es wird sonnig den ganzen Tag	It will be sunny all day

Fotografieren (taking photographs)

Ich muß eine Kassette in meinen Fotoapparat einlegen	I must put a cartridge in my camera
das Foto, das Bild	photo, picture
der Fotoapparat/die Kamera	camera
Einen Film mit vierundzwanzig Aufnahmen, bitte	A film with 24 exposures, please
einen Film entwickeln	to develop a film

Up and down

aufsteigen	to climb up	**bergauf**	uphill
absteigen	to climb down	**bergab**	downhill
hinauf	up, upwards, up there	**oben**	above, at the top
hinab	down, downwards, down there	**unten**	below, beneath, at the foot

the way it works

Plural nouns after mit, etc.

eine Landkarte **mit** Wanderweg**en**	a map with footpaths
die Berge, **mit** ihr**en** schneebedeckt**en** Gipfel**n**	the mountains, with their snowy peaks
Zelten wir **unter** den groß**en** Bäum**en**	We'll camp under the tall trees

Note the **n** at the end of the plural noun.

The castle that Ludwig built

Das Schloß, **das** Ludwig II gebaut hat	The castle that Ludwig II built
Die Abtei, **die** wir gestern besucht haben	The abbey which we visited yesterday
Der See, **den** Günther und Helen sehen wollen	The lake that Günther and Helen want to see
Die Ruinen, **die** wir besuchen wollen	The ruins that we want to visit

When the word for 'that', 'which' is the object of the clause, use **den** for a masculine noun in the singular.

things to do

7.1 You want to camp, but don't have much equipment. Can you ask the camp-shop assistant for what you need?

1 You'd like to hire a tent and two camp beds.
2 You need some camping gas for your stove.
3 You'd like to buy some matches and a water-bottle.
4 You'd like a battery for your torch.
5 Ask if there is drinking water in the tap.

7.2

Look at the weather map.

1 What is the weather like in Reykjavik?
2 What is it like in Lisbon?
3 What is it like in Paris and Frankfurt?
4 What kind of weather are they having in northern Scandinavia?
5 What is happening in Sicily?

Deutscher Wetterdienst

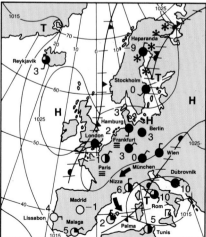

Vorhersagekarte
für den
30. Nov.

Zeichenerklärung:	
○	wolkenlos
◔	heiter
◑	halb bedeckt
◕	wolkig
●	bedeckt
↓	Nordwind 10 km/h
⟋	Ostwind 20 km/h
↑	Südwind 30 km/h
⟍●	Westwind 40 km/h
Temperatur in Grad Celsius	
≡	Nebel
∮	Sprühregen
●	Regen
∿	gefrierender Regen
✳	Schnee
▼	Schauer
℞	Gewitter
▨	Niederschlagsgebiet
▲▲	Warmfront
⌒⌒	Okklusion
▲▲	Kaltfront am Boden
△△	Kaltfront in der Höhe
⟹	Luftströmung warm
⟹	Luftströmung kalt
H	Hochdruckzentrum
T	Tiefdruckzentrum
h	Sekundär Hoch
t	Sekundär Tief
	Isobaren

SIGHTSEEING AND EXCURSIONS

Tourist information   For details of sightseeing tours and excursions, lists of local events and information about the many carnivals and festivals held during the tourist season (e.g. beer and music festivals in Germany), go to the **Fremdenverkehrsbüro** (tourist office). The staff will also assist you in booking accommodation, checking bus and train times, etc., and they have many brochures and leaflets, mostly free of charge. Tourist offices are located at main railway stations, or in town centres.

eine Stadtrundfahrt/a city tour

Ernst Fischer proposes to take George on a tour of the city on Sunday afternoon.

Ernst: Heute nachmittag **machen wir eine Stadtrundfahrt**, George. Wir werden alle Sehenswürdigkeiten anschauen – die Innenstadt, den Viktualienmarkt, das Siegestor, die Brunnen, das Schloß Nymphenburg . . .

George: Herrlich! **Ich muß auch einige Geschenke** für meine Frau und Jeremy, Helens Bruder in England, **kaufen**. Wo kann ich etwas für die Gegend Typisches finden?

Ernst: Fragen wir im Fremdenverkehrsbüro. (looking round as a young woman approaches) Aha, darf ich Ihnen Frau Gudrun Schulz, eine Mitarbeiterin vom Büro in Frankfurt, vorstellen. Frau Schulz ist Sekretärin des Geschäftsführers.

George: Schön, Sie kennenzulernen.

Ernst: Na, Gudrun, die Messe ist zu Ende! Sind Sie jetzt auf Urlaub?

Gudrun: Ja. **Ich möchte gern einen Ausflug ins Gebirge machen**, aber heute abend will ich **München bei Nacht sehen**.

George: München bei Nacht? Das klingt sehr interessant.

Gudrun: (to both) Möchten Sie gern mitkommen? Wir können alle drei zusammen gehen.

Ernst: Leider bin ich heute abend beschäftigt. Wie schade!

George: (hastily) Danke, ich komme sehr gern.

Gudrun: (turning to go) Also, bis heute abend – zwanzig Uhr am Karlsplatz.

Ernst: Tschüß, Gudrun.

George: Auf Wiedersehen, Frau Schulz. Bis heute abend!

Going on trips and excursions

Machen wir eine Rundfahrt	Let's go on a tour
eine Stadtrundfahrt	a tour of the town
Wir werden alle Sehenswürdigkeiten anschauen	We'll see all the sights
Besuchen wir . . .	Let's visit . . .
die Innenstadt/die Altstadt	the city centre/the old town
den Viktualienmarkt/das Siegestor	the victual market/the triumphal arch
die Brunnen/das Schloß Nymphenburg	the fountains/Nymphenburg castle
Ich bin auf Urlaub/geschäftlich hier	I am here on holiday/on business
Ich möchte gern einen Ausflug ins Gebirge machen	I'd love to go on an excursion to the mountains
Ich möchte München bei Nacht sehen	I'd like to see Munich by night

Making tourist enquiries

Ich muß einige Geschenke/Souvenirs kaufen	I must buy some presents/souvenirs
Wo ist das Reisebüro?	
Wo kann ich etwas für die Gegend Typisches finden?	Where can I find something typical of the region?
Fragen wir im Fremdenverkehrsbüro	We'll ask in the tourist office
Wo ist die Informationsstelle?	Where is the information office?
der Verkehrsverein/das Verkehrsamt?	the tourist bureau?
Haben Sie einen Reiseführer?	Do you have a guidebook?

73

Introducing a colleague

Darf ich Ihnen Frau Schulz vorstellen?	May I introduce Frau Schulz?
eine Mitarbeiterin vom Büro in Frankfurt	a colleague from the Frankfurt office
Schön, Sie kennenzulernen	Pleased to meet you
kennenlernen	to get to know
Sie ist Sekretärin des Geschäftsführers.	She's the manager's secretary
Sie arbeitet in einem Büro	She works in an office
Ich bin . . .	I'm a/an . . .
(For a list of jobs and workplaces, see p 81)	
Helens Bruder in England	Helen's brother in England
Das klingt interessant	That sounds interesting
alle drei zusammen	all three together
Ich bin beschäftigt	I'm busy
Tschüß	Goodbye (familiar)

the way it works

Possession

The director's secretary; the secretary of the director.
In German, there is a special way of saying 'of the', ' 's'.

die Sekretärin **des** Direktor**s** (m)	the director's secretary
der Chef **der** Fabrik (f)	the head of the factory
der Geschäftsführer **des** Hotel**s** (n)	the manager of the hotel

When talking about people, use an **s** without an apostrophe:

Gisela ist Karl-Heinrich**s** Schwester	Gisela is Karl-Heinrich's sister
Jeremy ist Helen**s** Bruder	Jeremy is Helen's brother

The same endings are also used after **während** (during) and **wegen** (because of), and nouns taking these endings are said to be in the genitive (possessive) case.

things to do

7.3 You go into a **Fremdenverkehrsbüro** in Germany.
1 Ask if they have a guidebook of the town.
2 Ask where you can buy some souvenirs for your family.
3 Ask if there is a tour of the city you can go on.
4 Say you'd like to go on an excursion to the mountains.
5 Ask if there is a travel agency nearby.

7.4 *Was sind sie von Beruf?*
What do these people do for a living?

1 Ich arbeite in einer Schule.
  Ah, Sie sind Lehrer!
2 Ich arbeite in einer Bank
  . . . .
3 Ich arbeite in einem Büro.
  . . . .

4 Ich arbeite in einem Krankenhaus.
  . . . .
5 Ich arbeite in einer Garage.
  . . . .

KEY TO EXERCISES

1.1 1 Ja, ich bin Herr Lowe. 2 Nein, ich bin Fräulein Leclerc. 3 Nein, ich heiße Tyler. 4 Ja, ich bin Herr Garcia. 5 Nein, ich heiße Brown. . . . Ich heiße/Ich bin/ Mein Name ist . . .
1.2 1 Guten Tag, Herr Schneider. Wie. geht's? 2 Guten Morgen, Frau Schwarz. 3 Guten Abend. . . Sehr erfreut. 4 Guten Tag. Wie geht es Ihnen?
1.3 2 . . . meine Mutter. 3 . . . ist mein Bruder. 4 . . . ist meine Schwester. . . . Das ist Ludwig, mein Mann/Das ist Thomas, mein Sohn/Das ist Gisela, meine Tochter/Das ist Karl-Heinrich, mein Sohn.
1.4 1 Ich möchte ein Einzelzimmer. 2 – ein Einzelzimmer mit Fernsehen. 3 – ein Doppelzimmer mit Bad. 4 – ein Zimmer mit zwei Betten, mit Balkon. 5 – ein Einzelzimmer mit Frühstück/ Übernachtung mit Frühstück.
1.5 1 Nein, für eine Person. 2 Nein, ich bleibe zwei Nächte. 3 Nein, ich möchte ein Zimmer nach vorn. 4 Es kostet zweihundertfünfzig DM pro Tag. zweihundertfünfzig DM pro Tag.
1.6 2 Er kommt aus England. 3 Er kommt aus der Schweiz. 4 Er kommt aus Österreich. 5 Sie kommt aus Amerika.

2.1 2 Spiegeleier mit Speck, Toast mit Honig, schwarzen Kaffee. 3 Schwarzbrot, Schinken, Tee mit Zitrone. 4 Orangensaft, ein Stück Toast mit Apfelsinenmarmelade, eine Tasse Tee mit Milch. 5 Brot, Käse, heiße Schokolade.
2.2 DM9,50.
2.3 1 Aber sie ist zu eng. 2 Aber sie sind zu teuer. 3 Ich habe die Farbe nicht gern. 4 Ich nehme es.
2.4 1 Ich esse lieber ein Schinkenbrot mit Kartoffelchips. 2 Ich esse lieber ein Omelett mit Käse, und Pommes Frites. 3 Ich esse lieber ein deutsches Beefsteak mit Kartoffelsalat. 4 Ich esse lieber eine Currywurst.
2.5 1 Für ihn, ein Glas Altbier. 2 Für sie, ein Glas Weißwein. 3 Für sie, eine Karaffe Rosé. 4 Für ihn, ein Glas Apfelwein. 5 Für sie, ein Glas Tomatensaft. 6 Für ihn, ein Glas

Mineralwasser. 7 Für sie, eine Flasche Whisky.

3.1 1 The museum. 2 The bank. 3 The hospital.
3.2 2 Sie gehen am besten zu Fuß. 3 Sie fahren am besten mit dem Bus. 4 Sie fahren am besten mit dem Zug. 5 Sie fahren am besten mit dem Bus/Sie gehen am besten zu Fuß. 6 Sie gehen am besten zu Fuß.
3.3 1 Wann fährt der nächste Zug nach Frankfurt? 2 Von welchem Gleis? 3 Muß ich umsteigen? 4 Wann/Um wieviel Uhr kommt der Zug an? 5 Kann ich einen Sitzplatz reservieren?
4.1 1 (a), 2 (a), 3 (c), 4 (c).
4.2 1 Ich möchte fünfzig Pfund in Deutsche Mark wechseln. 2 Ich möchte einen Reisescheck einlösen. 3 Wie ist der Wechselkurs heute? 4 Kann ich einen Euroscheck einlösen? Mein Paß ist im Hotel, aber ich habe eine Scheckkarte oder eine Kreditkarte.
4.3 1 Postlagernde Sendung. 2 Was kostet ein Brief nach England, bitte? 3 Drei Briefmarken zu siebzig Pfennig, bitte. 4 Ich möchte ein Paket in die Vereinigten Staaten/nach New York schicken. Was macht das, bitte? 5 Ich möchte eine Internationale Postanweisung einlösen. 6 Wieviel kostet eine Postkarte nach Australien?

5.1 1 Dreißig Liter Super, bitte. 2 Kann ich den Reifendruck prüfen, bitte? 3 Bitte prüfen Sie die Batterie. 4 Führen Sie Reparaturen aus?
5.2 1 Ich möchte ein kleines Auto/ einen kleinen Wagen mieten. 2 Wieviel kostet es für zwei Tage? 3 Muß ich eine Kautionssumme zahlen? 4 Ich möchte den Wagen in Stuttgart lassen. 5 Ich nehme den blauen Volkswagen. Geben Sie mir bitte den Schlüssel.
5.3 1 Ausfahrt. 2 (b). 3 (b).
5.4 A Nein, hier Helen Jackson/Helen Jackson am Apparat . . . Einen Augenblick, bitte–das tut mir leid, sie ist nicht hier . . . Sie kommt um halb sechs wieder zurück, glaube ich . . . Auf

Wiederhören. B Ich möchte Thomas sprechen, bitte . . . Hier Helen Jackson/ Helen Jackson am Apparat . . . Nein, ich rufe wieder an . . . Auf Wiederhören.

5.5 1 Er hat Magenschmerzen. 2 Sie hat Schmerzen im Fuß. 3 Er hat Kopfschmerzen. 4 Sie hat im Rücken Schmerzen/Der Rücken tut ihr weh. 5 Er hat Zahnschmerzen.

5.6 1 (a). 2 (a) Wo ist die nächste Apotheke? (b) Ich habe mich übergen. Haben Sie etwas gegen Magen-schmerzen? (c) Ich habe mir den Finger verbrannt und ich möchte ein Schmerzmittel. Brauche ich ein Rezept? (d) Wie oft soll ich die Tabletten einnehmen? (e) Ich möchte auch Antiseptikum und Watte. 3 (c).

5.7 1 (a), 2 (c), 3 (b).

5.8 Sleeping pills.

6.1 1(c), 2(f), 3(a), 4(b), 5(d), 6(e).

6.2 1 (c), 2 Ski sticks.

6.3 1 16 Marks. 2 10 minutes in the solarium. 3 Family, friends and acquaintances.

6.4 1 Recently (newly opened). 2 In the heart of the city. (Opposite the Münchner Hof Hotel in Goethestraße.) 3 Every day from 8 p.m.

6.5 e.g. 2 Sie will ein Konzert hören. 3 Er würde gern ins/zum Kino gehen. 4 Sie will tanzen gehen.

6.6 A 1 Um wieviel Uhr endet das Konzert? 2 Gibt es eine Ermäßigung für Studenten? 3 Ich möchte zwei Plätze im Balkon, nach vorn, bitte.
B 1 Der Eintrittspreis ist drei Mark. 2 Die Öffnungszeiten sind von elf bis achtzehn Uhr. 3 Es ist am Montag geschlossen.
C 1 Um wieviel Uhr beginnt die Vorstellung? 2 Kann ich die Plätze reservieren? 3 Einen Platz im Parkett/ Einmal Parkett, bitte.

7.1 1 Ich möchte ein Zelt und zwei Zeltbetten mieten. 2 Ich brauche Camping-Gas für meinen Kocher. 3 Ich möchte Streichhölzer und eine Wasserflasche kaufen/Geben Sie mir bitte . . . 4 Ich möchte auch eine Batterie für meine Taschenlampe. 5 Ist das Trinkwasser im Wasserhahn?

7.2 1 Cloudy, 3°. 2 Clear skies, 4°. 3 Paris: fairly cloudy, −1°; Frankfurt: completely overcast, 3°. 4 Cloudy, with snow. 5 Thunderstorms.

7.3 1 Haben Sie einen Reiseführer von der Stadt? 2 Wo kann ich einige Souvenirs für meine Familie kaufen? 3 Gibt es eine Stadtrundfahrt? 4 Ich möchte einen Ausflug ins Gebirge machen. 5 Gibt es eine Reisebüro in der Nähe?

7.4 2 Ah, Sie sind Bankbeamte/in. 3 Ah, Sie sind Sekretärin/Geschäftsmann/ frau, etc. 4 Ah, Sie sind Arzt/ Krankenschwester. 5 Ah, Sie sind Mechaniker.

English–German topic vocabularies

Months of the year (Die Monate)

January	**Januar**	May	**Mai**	September	**September**
February	**Februar**	June	**Juni**	October	**Oktober**
March	**März**	July	**Juli**	November	**November**
April	**April**	August	**August**	December	**Dezember**

in July	**im Juli**	next week	**nächste Woche**
last month	**im letzten Monat**	last year	**letztes Jahr**
last week	**letzte Woche**	next year	**nächstes Jahr**
next month	**im nächsten Monat**	this year	**dieses Jahr**

The seasons (Die Jahreszeiten)

spring	**der Frühling**	autumn	**der Herbst**
summer	**der Sommer**	winter	**der Winter**

The time (Die Zeit)

day	**der Tag (-e)**	year	**das Jahr (-e)**
month	**der Monat (-e)**	clock	**die Uhr (-en)**
week	**die Woche (-n)**	hour	**die Stunde (-n)**
weekend	**das Wochenende (-n)**	minute	**die Minute (-n)**
		second	**die Sekunde (-n)**

Numbers 1-1000

1	**eins**	6	**sechs**	11	**elf**	16	**sechzehn**
2	**zwei**	7	**sieben**	12	**zwölf**	17	**siebzehn**
3	**drei**	8	**acht**	13	**dreizehn**	18	**achtzehn**
4	**vier**	9	**neun**	14	**vierzehn**	19	**neunzehn**
5	**fünf**	10	**zehn**	15	**fünfzehn**	20	**zwanzig**

21	**einundzwanzig**	29	**neunundzwanzig**	80	**achtzig**
22	**zweiundzwanzig**	30	**dreißig**	90	**neunzig**
23	**dreiundzwanzig**	31	**einunddreißig**	100	**hundert**
24	**vierundzwanzig**	40	**vierzig**	101	**hunderteins**
25	**fünfundzwanzig**	50	**fünfzig**	200	**zweihundert**
26	**sechsundzwanzig**	60	**sechzig**	500	**fünfhundert**
27	**siebenundzwanzig**	70	**siebzig**	1000	**tausend**

Ordinal numbers

the first	**der erste**	the tenth	**der zehnte**
the second	**der zweite**	the 20th	**der zwanzigste**
the third	**der dritte**	the 21st	**der einundzwanzigste**
the fourth	**der vierte**	the 30th	**der dreißigste**
the fifth	**der fünfte**	the 50th	**der füngzigste**
the sixth	**der sechste**	the 82nd	**der zweiundachzigste**
the seventh	**der siebente/siebte**	the 100th	**der hundertste**
the eighth	**der achte**	the 1000th	**der tausendste**
the ninth	**der neunte**		

Der wievielte ist heute?	What's the date today?
Heute ist der fünfte Juni	It's the 5th of June

VOCABULARY

Clothes (Die Kleidung)

anorak	der Anorak (-s)
blouse	die Bluse (-n)
blouson	der Blouson
boots	die Steifel (pl.)
bra	der Büstenhalter (-)/BH
briefs	der Schlüpfer (-)
cardigan	die Wolljacke (-n)
coat	der Mantel (¨)
dress	das Kleid (-er)
gloves	die Handschuhe (pl.)
hat	der Hut (¨e)
jacket	die Jacke (-n)
jeans	die Jeans (pl.)
nightdress	das Nachthemd (-en)
pullover	der Pullover (-)
pyjamas	der Schlafanzug (¨e)
raincoat	der Regenmantel (¨)

scarf	das Halstuch (¨er)
shirt	das Hemd (-en)
shoes	die Schuhe (pl.)
skirt	der Rock (¨e)
socks	die Socken (pl.)
stockings	die Strümpfe (pl.)
suit (man's)	der Anzug (¨e)
sweatshirt	das Sweatshirt (-s)
swimming costume	der Badeanzug (¨e)
tee-shirt	das T-shirt (-s)
tie	die Krawatte (-n)
tights	die Strumpfhose (-n)
tracksuit	der Trainingsanzug (¨e)
trainers	die Turnschuhe (pl.)
trousers	die Hose (-n)
underpants	die Unterhose (-n)/der Slip (-s)

Colours (Die Farben)

black	schwarz	purple	purpur
blue	blau	red	rot
brown	braun	white	weiß
green	grün	yellow	gelb
grey	grau	dark	dunkel
pink	rosa	light	hell

Materials (Die Stoffe)

cotton	Baumwolle	nylon	Nylon
denim	Stoff	silk	Seide
leather	Leder	suede	Wildleder
linen	Leinen	wool	Wolle

At the chemist's

antiseptic	das Antiseptikum
bandage	der Verband (¨e)
cotton wool	die Watte
cough syrup	der Hustensaft
eye drops	die Augentropfen
laxative	das Abführmittel
medicine	die Medizin (-)

painkiller	das Schmerzmittel
pill	die Pille (-n)
plaster	das Heftpflaster
tablet	die Tablette (-n)
thermometer	das Thermometer
throat pills	die Halspastillen

Toiletries (Die Toilettenartikel)

aftershave	das Rasierwasser
baby food	die Babynahrung (-)
brush	die Bürste (-n)
comb	der Kamm (¨e)
contact lens cleaner	der Kontaktlins-enreiniger
contraceptives	die Verhütungsmittel
cream	die Creme (-s)
deodorant	das Deodorant
disposable nappies	die Wegwerf-Windeln
perfume	das Parfüm (-e)
razor	der Rasierapparat (-e)
razor blades	die Rasierklingen
safety pins	die Sicherheitsnadel

sanitary towels	die Damenbinden
shampoo	das Haarwaschmittel (-)
shaving cream	die Rasiercreme
soap	die Seife (-n)
suntan lotion	die Sonnenmilch
talc	das Körperpuder (-)
tampons	die Tampons
tissues	die Papiertücher
toothbrush	die Zahnbürste (-n)
toothpaste	die Zahnpasta

VOCABULARY

Food

Fish (Der Fisch)

carp	der Karpfen (-)	mackerel	die Makrele (-n)
cod	der Kabeljau (-e)	plaice	die Scholle (-n)
crab	der Krebs (-e)	prawns	die Garnelen (pl.)
eel	der Aal (-e)	salmon	der Lachs (-e)
haddock	der Schellfisch (-e)	shrimps	die Krabben (pl.)
halibut	der Heilbutt (-e)	sole	die Seezunge (-n)
herring	der Hering (-e)	trout	die Forelle (-n)
lobster	der Hummer (-)	tuna	der Thunfisch (-e)

Meat (Das Fleisch)

chop	das Kotelett (-s)		
escalope	das Schnitzel (-)	well done	durchgebraten
kidneys	die Nieren	veal	das Kalbfleisch
liver	die Leber	breaded veal	Weiener Schnitzel
steak	das Steak (-s)	escalope	
beef	das Rindfleisch	lamb	das Hammelfleisch/
braised beef	der Rostbraten		der Lamm
goulash	das Gulasch	lamb chop	das Lammkotelett
meat loaf	der Hackbraten	roast lamb	der Lammbraten
mince	das Hackfleisch	pork	das Schweinefleisch
rib steak	das Rippensteak	bacon	der Speck
steak	das Filetsteak	ham	der Schinken
rare	blutig	knuckle of pork	das Eisbein
medium	mittel/medium	spare ribs	die Rippchen

Poultry and game (Das Geflügel und das Wild)

chicken	das Hähnchen (-)/	partridge	das Rebhuhn (¨er)
	das Huhn (¨er)	pheasant	der Fasan (-e)
duck	die Ente (-n)	pigeon	die Taube (-n)
goose	die Gans (¨e)	rabbit	das Kaninchen (-)
hare	der Hase (-n)	turkey	der Truthahn (¨e)

Vegetables (Die Gemüse)

asparagus	der Spargel (-)	mushroom	der Pilz (-e)
aubergine	die Aubergine	noodles	die Nudeln (pl.)
bean	die Bohne (-n)	onion	die Zwiebel (-n)
broccoli	der Braunkohl (-e)	pea	die Erbse (-n)
cabbage	der Kohl (-e)	potato	die Kartoffel (-n)
pickled cabbage	das Sauerkraut (¨er)	boiled	Salzkartoffeln
carrot	die Karotte (-n)	boiled in skins	Pellkartoffeln
cauliflower	der Blumenkohl (-e)	mashed	der Kartoffelbrei
celery	die Sellerie	roast	Bratkartoffeln
courgettes	die Zucchetti (pl.)	radishes	die Radieschen (pl.)
cucumber	die Salatgurke (-n)	red cabbage	das Blaukraut/
dumplings	die Klöße/die Knödel (pl.)		der Rotkohl
garlic	der Knoblauch	spinach	der Spinat (-e)
gherkin	die Essiggurke (-n)	sprouts	der Rosenkohl (sing.)
gnocchi	die Spätzle (pl.)	sweetcorn	der Mais
leek	der Lauch (-e)	tomato	die Tomate (-n)
lettuce	der Kopfsalat (-e)	turnip	der Kohlrabi

VOCABULARY

Fruit (Das Obst)

apple	der Apfel (die Äpfel)
apricot	die Aprikose (-n)
banana	die Banane (-n)
blackberry	die Brombeere (-n)
cherry	die Kirsche (-n)
grapefruit	die Pampelmuse (-n)
grape	die Traube (-n)
lemon	die Zitrone (-n)
orange	die Apfelsine (-n)
peach	der Pfirsich (-e)
pear	die Birne (-n)
pineapple	die Ananas (-)
plum	die Pflaume (-n)
raspberry	die Himbeere (-n)
red/ blackcurrants	Rote/Schwarze Johannisbeeren (pl.)
rhubarb	der Rhabarber
strawberry	die Erdbeere (-n)

Weather (Das Wetter)

clear	heiter
cloudless	wolkenlos
cloudy	wolkig
drizzle	der Sprühregen
fog	der Nebel
hail	der Hagel
ice	das Eis
lightning	der Blitz (-e)
rain	der Regen
rainfall	der Niederschlag
shower	der Schauer (-)
snow	der Schnee
storm	der Sturm (¨e)
thunder	der Donner (-)
thunderstorm	das Gewitter (-)

Car parts

accelerator	das Gaspedal	ignition	die Zündung
boot	der Kofferraum	indicators	die Blinker
brakes	die Bremsen	lights	die Scheinwerfer
bulb	die Glühbirne	numberplate	das Nummernschild
bumper	die Stoßstange	plugs	die Zündkerzen
carburettor	der Vergaser	radiator	der Kühler
clutch	die Kupplung	seatbelt	der Sicherheitsgurt (-e)
dynamo	die Lichtmaschine	starter	der Anlasser
engine	der Motor	steering wheel	das Lenkrad
exhaust	der Auspuff	tyres	die Reifen
fan-belt	der Keilriemen	wheel	das Rad (¨er)
fuses	die Sicherungen	windscreen	die Windschutz- scheibe
gear box	das Getriebe		
horn	die Hupe	wipers	die Scheibenwischer

Sport (Der Sport)

archery	das Bogenschießen	jogging	der Jogging
badminton	der Federball	judo	das Judo
basketball	der Basketball	racing	das Autorennen
bathing	das Baden	riding	das Reiten
billiards	das Billardspiel	rollerskating	das Rollschuhlaufen
chess	das Schachspielen	rugby	das Rugby
climbing	das Bergsteigen	sailing	das Segeln
cycling	das Radfahren	shooting	das Schießen
fishing	das Angeln	skating	das Schlittschuhlaufen
football	der Fußball	skiing	das Skifahren
golf	das Golf	swimming	das Schwimmen
handball	der Handball	tennis	das Tennis
hang-gliding	das Drachenfliegen	volleyball	der Volleyball
hiking, walking	das Wandern	water-skiing	das Wasserskifahren
hockey	das Hockey	wind-surfing	das Windsurfen
horse-racing	das Pferderennen	winter sports	der Wintersport
hunting	die Jagd	yoga	der Yoga

VOCABULARY

Parts of the body

arm	der Arm (-e)	hand	die Hand (¨e)
back	der Rücken (-)	head	der Kopf (¨e)
body	der Körper (-)	heart	der Herz (-en)
blood	das Blut	knee	das Knie (-n)
breast	die Brust (¨e)	lip	die Lippe (-n)
chest	der Brustkorb (¨er)	leg	das Bein (-e)
ear	das Ohr (-en)	mouth	der Mund (¨er)
elbow	der Ellbogen (-)	neck	der Hals (¨e)
eye	das Auge (-n)	nose	die Nase (-n)
face	das Gesicht (-er)	shoulder	die Schulter (-n)
finger	der Finger (-)	stomach	der Magen (-)
foot	der Fuß (Füße)	toe	die Zehe (-n)
hair	das Haar (-e)	tongue	die Zunge (-n)

Jobs (Die Arbeit)

accountant/bank clerk	Buchhalter/Bankbeamte, -beamtin
businessman, businesswoman	Geschäftsmann, Geschäftsfrau
chef	Küchenchef, -chefin
computer programmer	Computer-Programmierer, -erin
director/doctor	Direktor/Arzt
engineer	Ingenieur
factory worker	Fabrikarbeiter, -erin
fashion designer	Mode-Designer, -erin
head of a firm/company	Chef, Chefin einer Firma/Gesellschaft
housewife/journalist	Hausfrau/Journalist, -istin
lab assistant/lawyer	Laborant, -antin/Rechtsanwalt
lecturer/manager	Dozent, -entin/Geschäftsführer
mechanic/nurse	Mechaniker/Krankenschwester
painter	Maler
sales assistant	Verkäufer, -erin
(sales) representative	Handelsvertreter, -erin
student/teacher	Student, -entin/Lehrer, -erin
technician/writer	Techniker/Schriftsteller, -erin

Workplaces

I work in a/an . . .	**Ich arbeite in einem**		**. . . in einer**
		bank	Bank
hospital	Krankenhaus	college	Hochschule
hotel	Hotel	factory	Fabrik
laboratory	Laboratorium	garage	Garage
office	Büro	school	Schule
shop	Laden	university	Universität
studio	Atelier	workshop	Werkstatt

Leisure and entertainment

art gallery	die Kunstgalerie (-n)	film	der Film (-e)
ballet	das Ballett (-e)	monument	das Denkmal (¨e)
casino	das Kasino (-s)	museum	das Museum (-een)
cathedral	der Dom (-e)	nightclub	der Nachtclub (-s)
cinema	das Kino (-s)	opera	die Oper (-n)
concert	das Konzert (-e)	play	das Theaterstück (-e)
discotheque	die Diskothek (-s)	theatre	das Theater (-)

VOCABULARY

German–English

Plurals of nouns are given in brackets where appropriate, e.g. **der Anzug** (¨e) – die Anzüge.

ab from

Abend *m.* (-e) evening; **am-** in the evening; **guten-** good evening; **abends** in the evening; **-essen** *n.* dinner, supper

aber but

abfahren leave, depart

Abfahrt *f.* (-en) departure

absteigen climb down

Abtei *f.* (-en) abbey

Abteil *n.* (-e) compartment

Adresse *f.* (-n) address

all/aller/alle/alles all, every, everything

allergisch allergic

als when, than

also so, then, well then

alt old; **Altbier** *n.* bitter; **Altstadt** *f.* (¨e) old town

am at the

Amerika *n.* America

Amerikaner *m.* (-)/**erin** *f.* (-innen) American (person)

amerikanisch American

Ampel *f.* (-n) traffic lights

an (+ acc./dat.) at, to, on

anfangen begin

Angeln *n.* fishing

Angelrute *f.* (-n) fishing rod

angenehm pleasant(ly)

Angestellte(r) *f. m.* (-n, -en) employee

ängstlich anxious

ankommen arrive; **es kommt darauf an** that depends

Ankunft *f.* (¨e) arrival

Anorak *m.* (-s) anorak

anprobieren try on

anrufen phone, ring up

anschauen look at

Anschlagbrett *n.* (-er) notice board

ansehen look at

anspringen start (car)

antworten reply

Anzug *m.* (¨e) suit (man's)

Apfel *m.* (¨) apple; **-wein** *m.* (-e) cider

Apfelsine *f.* (-n) orange

Apfelsinenmarmelade *f.* (-n) marmalade

Apotheke *f.* (-n) chemist's; **Apotheker** *m.* (-) chemist

Apparat *m.* (-e) camera, telephone; **am-** on the phone

Appetit *m.* appetite; **guten -!** bon appétit!

Arbeit *f.* (-en) work; **arbeiten** work; **arbeitslos** unemployed

ärgerlich cross, angry

arm poor

Arm *m.* (-e) arm

Arzt *m.* (¨e) doctor

atmen breathe

auch too, also

auf (+ acc./dat.) on, in, at; **- Wiedersehen!** goodbye!

aufgeben send (telegram)

Aufnahme *f.* (-n) exposure (film)

aufpassen: paß auf! look out!

aufsteigen climb (up)

Aufzug *m.* (¨e) lift

Auge *n.* (-n) eye

Augenblick *m.* (-e) moment

aus (+ dat.) from, out of

Ausfahrt *f.* (-en) exit

Ausflug *m.* (¨e) excursion; **einen – machen** go on an excursion

ausführen carry out

ausfüllen fill in, up

ausgehen stall (engine)

ausgezeichnet excellent(ly)

Auskunft *f.* (¨e) information

Ausland *n.* abroad

ausrichten: kann ich etwas – ? can I take a message?

ausruhen, sich rest

Ausrüstung *f.* (-en) equipment

aussehen look, seem

ausstehen: nicht - loathe

außer (+ dat.) besides

Aussicht *f.* (-en) view

Ausstellung *f.* (-en) exhibition; **-shalle** *f.* (-n) exhibition hall

Auto *n.* (-s) car; **(-bahn** *f.* (-en) motorway; **-vermietung** *f.* (-en) car hire office/ service

Automat *m.* (-en) slot machine

VOCABULARY

Bäckerei *f.* (-e) baker's
Bad *n.* (¨er) bath; **-eanzug** *m.* (¨e) bathing costume; **-ezimmer** *n.* (-) bathroom
baden bathe
Bahnbeamte(r)/in *f. m.* (-, innen) railway employee
Bahnhof *m.* (¨e) station
Bahnsteig *m.* (-e) platform
bald soon; **bis -** see you later
Ball *m.* (¨e) ball
Ballett *n.* (-e) ballet
Balkon *m.* (-e) balcony; circle (cin.)
Banane *f.* (-n) banana
Bank *f.* (-en) bank; **-beamte(r)/in** *m., f.* (-, innen) bank clerk
Bar *f.* (-s) bar
Bargeld *n.* cash
Batterie *f.* (-e) battery
bauen build
Bauernhof *m.* (¨e) farm
Baum *m.* (¨e) tree
Bayern *n.* Bavaria; **bayerisch** Bavarian
bedeckt overcast
Bedienung *f.* (-en) service
beginnen begin
bei *(+ dat.)* near, at, at the house of
Bein *n.* (-e) leg
Beispiel: zum - (z.B.) for example
Bekannte(r) *m., f.* acquaintance
bekommen get, receive
Benzin *n.* petrol
beraten advise
bereit ready
bergab downhill; **bergauf** uphill
Berg *m.* (-e) mountain, hill; **-steigen** *n.* climbing
Beruf *m.* (-e) job, profession; **von -** by profession
beruhigen calm
berühmt famous
beschäftigt busy, occupied
besetzt occupied, engaged
besonders especially
Bestätigung *f.* (-e) confirmation
bestellen order
besten: am - best
bestimmt right, certain
Besuch *m.* (-e) visit
besuchen visit
Bett *n.* (-en) bed
bewaldet wooded
bewegen move

bezahlen pay
Bier *n.* (-) beer; **-keller** *m.* (-) ale-house; **-stube** *f.* (-n) pub
Bild *n.* (-er) picture, photo
billig cheap
bin: *see* **sein**
Birne *f.* (-n) pear
bißchen: ein - a little, bit
bitte please; **-?** pardon?; **- schön!** don't mention it!
blau blue
bleiben stay, remain
blöd stupid
Bluse *f.* (-n) blouse
Blut *n.* blood; **blutig** rare (steak)
Boden *m.* (¨) ground, floor
Bogenschießen *n.* archery
Bohne *f.* (-n) bean
Boot *n.* (-e) boat
Botschaft *f.* (-en) embassy
Bratwurststand *m.* (¨e) sausage stall
brauchen need
braun brown
Bremse *f.* (-n) brake
Brief *m.* (-e) letter; **-kasten** *m.* (¨) letter box; **-marke** *f.* (-n) stamp; **-tasche** *f.* (-n) wallet
Brille *f.* (-n) glasses
bringen bring
Broschüre *f.* (-n) brochure
Brot *n.* (-e) bread, loaf
Brötchen *n.* (-) roll
Brücke *f.* (-n) bridge
Bruder *m.* (¨) brother
Brunnen *m.* (-) fountain, well
Buch *n.* (¨e) book
Büchse *f.* (-n) can, tin
Bucht *f.*(-en) bay
Burg *f.* (-en) fortress, castle
Bus *m.* (-se) bus; **-haltestelle** *f.* (-n) bus stop

Café *n.* (-s) café
campen camp; **Campingladen** *m.* (¨) camp shop
Chef/Chefin *m., f.* (-s, innen) boss, chief
Chor *m.* (¨e) choir

da there, then; **- drüben** over there
Dach *n.* (¨er) roof
Dame *f.* (-n) lady; **Damen** ladies (toilets)
Dank: vielen - many thanks; **danke schön** thank you very much

danken thank
dann then
darf: *see* **dürfen**
das the, that; **- ist** that is
daß that
Datum *n.* (**Daten**) date
dauern last
denken think
Denkmal *n.* (¨e) monument
den the
denn for, because
der the
deutsch German; **Deutschland** *n.*
　Germany; **Deutschmark** *f.* (-) Mark
dich (*acc.*) you (fam.)
die the
dieser/e/es this, that
dir (*dat.*) (to) you (fam.)
Direktor *m.* (-en) manager
Dirigent *m.* (-en) conductor
doch yes (after neg.)
Dom *m.* (-e) cathedral
Doppelzimmer *n.* (-) double room
Dorf *n.* (¨er) village
dort there
Dose *f.* (-n) tin, can; **-nöffner** *m.* (-) can
　opener
Dragee *n.* (-s) pastel, pill
Droge *f.* (-n) drug; **Drogerie** *f.* (-n)
　chemist's, drugstore
du you (fam.)
dunkel dark
D-Zug (Durchgangszug) *m.* (¨e) express
　train
durch (+ *acc.*) through; **-gebraten** well
　done (steak)
dürfen may, be allowed to
Durst *m.* thirst; **- haben** be thirsty
Dusche *f.* (-n) shower
Dutzend *n.* (-e) dozen
eben even, just
Ecke *f.* (-n) corner; **in der -** in the corner
Ei *n.* (-er) egg
ein/eine/einen/eins a, one;
　Einbahnstraße *f.* (-n) one-way street
einfach single (ticket)
Einfahrt *f.* (-en) entrance (motorway)
Eingang *m.* (¨e) entrance
einige some
Einkauf *m.* (¨e) purchase; **Einkäufe**
　machen go shopping
einlösen cash (cheque, etc.)
einmal once

einlegen put in, insert
einsteigen get in (train, etc.)
eintragen, sich register
Eintritt *m.* entrance, entry; **-skarte** *f.* (-n)
　entrance ticket; **-spreis** *m.* (-e)
　entrance fee
Einzelfahrkarte *f.* (-n) single ticket
Einzelzimmer *n.* (-) single room
Eis *n.* ice, ice cream; **-bahn** *f.* (-en)
　skating rink; **-becher** *m.* ice cream
　sundae; **-sporthalle** *f.* (-n) ice stadium
Eisbein *n.* leg of pork
Eltern *pl.* parents
Empfang *m.* (¨e) reception; **-sdame** *f.*
　(-n) receptionist
empfehlen recommend
Ende: zu - at an end, finished
endlich at last, finally
eng tight, narrow
England *n.* England
Engländer/erin *m., f.* (-, innen)
　Englishman/woman
englisch English
Ente *f.* (-n) duck
entfernt far
entlang (+ *acc.*) along
entschuldigen, sich excuse o.self; **- Sie**
　excuse me
entwickeln develop (film)
er he
Erbsen *pl.* peas
Erdgeschoß: im - on the ground floor
erfrieren freeze to death
erfreut pleased, glad
Ermäßigung *f.* (-en) reduction
ernst serious
erst first; **-mal** firstly
Erwachsene *pl.* adults
es it
essen eat; **Essen** *n.* meal, eating
Essig *m.* vinegar
etwas something, anything
Euroscheck *m.* (-s) Eurocheque

Fabrik *f.* (-en) factory
fahren go, drive, travel; **Fahrer** *m.* (-)
　driver
Fahrkarte, Fahrschein *f., m.* (-n, -e)
　ticket
Fahrrad *n.* (¨er) bicycle
Fahrt *f.* (-en) trip; **gute - !** have a good
　journey!
Familie *f.* (-n) family

Farbe *f.* (-n) colour
Fenster *n.* (-) window
Ferien *pl.* holidays: **in den** - on holiday
fern distant
Fernsehen *n.* TV
Fernsprecher *m.* (-) telephone box
fertig ready, finished
Fest *n.* (-e) festival
Feuer *n.* (-) fire; **-wache** *f.* fire station
Fieber *n.* fever
finden find
Finger *m.* (-) finger
Firma *m.* (-en) firm
Fisch *m.* (-e) fish; **-gericht** *n.* (-e) fish
 dish; **-handlung** *f.* (-en) fishmonger
Flasche *f.* (-n) bottle
Fleisch *n.* meat; (**-gerei** *f.* (en) butcher's;
 -speise *f.* (-n) meat dish
fliegen fly
Flug *m.* (¨e) flight; **-hafen** *m.* (¨) airport;
 -schein *m.* (-e) air ticket; **-zeug** *n.* (-e)
 aeroplane
Fluß *m.* (¨e) river
fördern promote, encourage
Forelle *f.* (-n) trout
Formular *n.* (-e) form
Foto *n.* (-s) photo; **fotografieren**
 photograph
fragen ask
französisch French
Frau *f.* (-en) woman, wife, Mrs
Fräulein *n.* (-) young lady, Miss;
 waitress
frei free; **Freibad** *n.* (¨er) open air pool
Fremdenverkehrsbüro *n.* (-s) tourist
 information offlce
freut: es - mich I like it
Freund *m.* (-e)/ **Freundin** *f.* (innen)
 friend; **freundlich** friendly
frieren freeze
frisch fresh
Fruchtsaft *m.* (¨e) fruit juice
Frühstück *n.* (-e) breakfast; **frühstücken**
 have breakfast
fühlen, sich feel
Führerschein *m.* (-e) driving licence
Fundamt *n.* (¨er)/ **Fundbüro** *n.* (-s) lost
 property office
furchtbar dreadful
Fuß *m.* (¨e) foot; **zu** -. on foot
Fußball *m.* (¨e) football; **-spiel** *n.* (-e)
 football match; **-platz** *m.* (¨e) football
 pitch
Fußgänger *m.* (-) pedestrian

Gabel *f.* (-n) fork
ganz quite, whole; **den -en Tag** all day
Garderobe *f.* (-n) cloakroom
Garten *m.* (¨) garden
Gast *m.* (¨e) guest; **-familie** *f.* (-n) host
 family
gebacken baked
Gebäude *n.* (-) building
geben give; **es gibt** there is/are
Gebirge *n.* (-) mountains
gebissen bitten
gebrochen broken
Gebühren *pl.* charges
Gefahr *f.* (-en) danger
gefallen please, like; **es gefällt mir** I like
 it
Gedeck *n.* (-e) set menu
gegen (+ *acc.*) about, against,
 to(wards), for; **-über** (+ *dat.*) opposite
Gegend *f.* (-en) district
gehen go, walk; **wie geht's?** how are
 you?; **es geht mir gut** I'm well
gekocht boiled
gelb yellow
Geld *n.* (-er) money; **-schein** *m.* (-e)
 banknote; **-strafe** *f.* (-n) fine
gemischt mixed
Gemüse *n.* (-) vegetable
gemütlich nice, cosy
genau exact(ly)
Gepäck *n.* luggage
gerade straight; **-aus** straight on
gern(e) willingly - **haben** to like
Geschäft *n.* (-e) shop, business; **-smann**/
 frau *m.*, *f.* (¨ er, -en) businessman/
 woman; **-sführer** *m.* (-) manager;
 -sreise *f.* (-n) business trip; **-sviertel** *n.*
 (-) business district
geschäftlich on business
Geschenk *n.* (-e) present, gift
geschlossen closed
geschwollen swollen
Gesellschaft *f.* (-en) company
Gesicht *n.* (-er) face
gestern yesterday
gestochen stung
gestohlen stolen
gesund healthy, well; **Gesundheit** *f.*
 (-en) health
Glas *n.* (¨er) glass
glauben think, believe; **ich glaube**
 schon I think so
gleich immediate(ly); **mir ist das** - it's all
 the same to me

Gleis *n.* (-e) platform, track
Golf *n.* golf; **-platz** *m.* (¨e) golf course
grau grey
Grenze *f.* (-n) border
groß big, large; **-artig** magnificent
grün green
gucken look; **guck mal!** look!
gut good, well

Haar *n.* (-e) hair; **-waschmittel** *n.* (-) shampoo
haben have
Hafen *m.* (¨) harbour, port
Hähnchen *n.* (-) chicken
halb half; **Halbpension** *f.* half board
Hallenbad *n.* (¨er) indoor pool
Hals *m.* (¨e) neck
halten keep, hold
Haltestelle *f.* (-n) bus stop
Hammelfleisch *n.* lamb (meat)
Hand *f.* (¨e) hand; **-tuch** *n.* (-e) towel; **-schuh** *m.* (-e) glove; **-tasche** *f.* (-n) handbag
hat: *see* **haben**
hätte: ich - gern I'd like
Hauptbahnhof *m.* (¨e) main station
Haus *n.* (¨er) house; **nach -e** home(wards); **zu-e** at home
heiß hot
heißen be called
heiter clear (sky)
hell light
helfen help
Hemd *n.* (-en) shirt
Hering *m.* (-e) tent peg
Herr *m.* (-en) gentleman, man, Mr; **-en** gents (toilets); **- Ober!** waiter!
herrlich lovely, splendid
herüber over (here)
Herz *n.* (-en) heart
heute today; **- abend** this evening
heutzutage nowadays
hier here
Hilfe *f.* help; **Erste -** first aid
Himmel *m.* (-) heaven
hin: - und zurück return (journey)
hinaufsteigen climb up
hinfallen fall down
hinten: nach - at the back, behind
hinter *(+ acc./dat.)* behind; **-lassen** leave behind
hoch high
hoffen hope
holen fetch, bring

Holzhammer *m.* (¨) mallet
homöopathisch homeopathic
Honig *m.* honey
hören hear
Hose *f.* (-n) trousers
Hotel *n.* (-s) hotel
Huhn *n.* (¨er) chicken
hundert hundred
Hunger *m.* hunger; **- haben** be hungry
Hupe *f.* (-n) horn
Husten *m.* (-) cough
Hut *m.* (¨e) hat
ich I
ihn *(acc.)* him
ihnen *(dat.)* them, to them
Ihnen *(dat.)* you, to you
ihr *(dat.)* her, to her; **-** *(adj.)* her, their
Ihr *(adj.)* your
im (in + dem) in the
immer always
in *(+ acc./dat.)* in, into, to, at
inbegriffen included
Informationstelle *f.* (-n) information office
Ingenieur *m.* (-e) engineer
Insel *f.* (-n) island
interessant interesting; **interessieren, sich (für)** be interested (in)
ist: *see* **sein**

ja yes
Jacke *f.* (-n) jacket coat
Jahr *n.* (-e) year; **-eszeit** *f.* (-en) season; **jährlich** annual
jeder/e/es every, each
jedermann everyone
jetzt now
Jugendherberge *f.* (-n) Youth Hostel
jung young
Junge *m.* (-n) boy

Kaffee *m.* (-s) coffee
kalt cold
Kalbfleisch *n.* veal
Kamm *m.* (¨er) comb
Kännchen *n.* (-) small pot
kann: *see* **können**
Kapelle *f.* (-n) band, chapel
kaputt broken
Karotte *f.* (-n) carrot
Karte *f.* (-n) ticket, card; menu
Kartoffel *f.* (-n) potato; **-chips** *pl.* crisps
Käse *m.* (-) cheese; **-kuchen** *m.* (-) cheesecake

VOCABULARY

Kasse *f.* (-n) cash desk, check-out
Kassette *f.* (-n) cassette, cartridge;
  -nrecorder cassette-recorder
kaufen buy; Kaufhaus *n.* (¨er)
  department store
kaum scarcely
Kautionssumme *f.* (-n) deposit
kein/keine/keines no, not any
Keks *m.* (-e) biscuit
Kellner/in *m.*, *f.* (-, innen) waiter,
  waitress
kennen know; -lernen get to know,
  meet
Kind *n.* (-er) child
Kino *n.* (-s) cinema
Kirche *f.* (-n) church
Kirsche *f.* (-n) cherry
Klasse *f.* (-n) class
Kleid *n.* (-er) dress
Kleidung *f.* clothes
klein little, small
Klima *n.* (-s) climate
klingen sound
Klinik *f.* (-en) clinic
Kloster *n.* (¨) monastery, convent
Knöchel *m.* (-) ankle
Kocher *m.* (-) stove
Koffer *m.* (-) bag, suitcase
Knödel *m.* (-) dumpling
Kohl *m.* (-) cabbage
Köln *n.* Cologne
kommen come
Komödie *f.* (-n) comedy
Konditorei *f.* (-en) cake shop, café
Konfitüre *f.* (-n) jam
können can, be able
Konsulat *n.* (-e) consulate
Konto *n.* (-ten) account (bank); -karte *f.*
  (-n) bank card
Konzert *n.* (-e) concert; -halle *f.* (-n)
  concert hall
Kopf *m.* (¨e) head; -salat *m.* (-) lettuce
Korkenzieher *m.* (-) corkscrew
Körper *m.* (-) body; -puder *m.* (-) talc
kosten cost
krank ill; Krankenhaus *n.* (¨er) hospital;
  Krankenschwester *f.* (-) nurse
Krawatte *f.* (-n) tie
Kreditkarte *f.* (-n) credit card
Kreisverkehr *m.* roundabout
Kreuzung *f.* (-en) crossing; cross roads
Kuchen *m.* (-) cake, pie
kühl cool
Kunde *m.* (-n) customer

Kunst *f.* (¨e) art; -galerie *f.* (-n) art
  gallery
Künstler *m.* (-) artist
kurz short; Kürz-film *m.* (-e) short film
Kusine *f.* (-n) (female) cousin

Land *n.* (¨er) country; -karte *f.* (-n) map;
  -schaft *f.* scenery, countryside
lang long; wie lange? how long?
langsam slow(ly)
langweilig boring
lassen let, leave
Lastkraftwagen *m.* (-) lorry
laufen run, show (film)
leben live; Diät - be on a diet
Lebensmittelgeschäft *n.* (-) grocer's
Leber *f.* liver; -wurst (¨e) liver sausage
leer empty
legen put, place
Lehrer *m.* (-) teacher
leicht light
leid: das tut mir - I'm sorry; leider
  unfortunately
leiden bear, stand
leihen hire
lernen learn
lesen read
letzt last; -es Jahr last year; -e Woche last
  week
Leute *pl.* people
lieb dear; Liebchen darling
lieber: ich habe - I prefer
liegen lie, be situated
Lift *m.* (-e) lift; -paß *m.* (¨e) lift pass
Limonade *f.* lemonade
Linie *f.* (-n) line, route
link left; -s on the left
Liste *f.* (-n) list
los: was ist los? what's the matter?
Londoner/in *m.*, *f.* (-, innen) Londoner
Luft *f.* (¨e) air
Luftmatratze *f.* (n) air bed, lilo
Lust: ich habe - I feel like

machen make, do; was macht das? what
  does that come to?
Mädchen *n.* (-) girl
mag: *see* mögen
Magen *m.* (¨) stomach; -schmerzen *pl.*
  stomach-ache
Mahlzeit *f.* (-en) meal
Mal *n.* (-e) time
mal just, only
Maler *m.* (-) painter, artist

man one, they, etc.
Mann *m.* (¨er) man
Mantel *m.* (¨) coat
Mark *f.* (-) Mark (curr.)
markiert marked
Markt *m.* (¨e) market
Marmelade *f.* (-n) jam
Maß *n.* (-e) measurement
Mauer *f.* (-n) wall
Mechaniker *m.* (-) mechanic
Medikament *n.* (-e) medicine
Medizin *f.* (-) medicine
Meer *n.* (-e) sea
Mehl *n.* (-e) flour
mehr more
Mehrwertsteuer *f.* VAT
mein/meine/meines my
Menü *n.* (-s) set menu
Messe *f.* (-n) fair; **-gelände** *n.* fair
   ground
Messer *n.* (-) knife
Metzgerei *f.* (-en) butcher's
mich *(acc.)* me
mieten hire
mild mild, calm
Mineralwasser *n.* (-) mineral water
mir *(dat.)* me, to me
mit *(+ dat.)* with; **-bringen** bring with;
   -gebracht brought with; **-kommen**
   come with, accompany
Mitarbeiter/in *m., f.* (-, innen) colleague
Mittag *m.* midday; **-essen** *n.* (-) lunch;
   -spause *f.* (-n) lunch break
Mittel *n.* (-) remedy, means
mittel medium
mitten in in the middle of
Mitternacht *f.* midnight
möchte: ich - I would like
mögen may, like
möglich possible
Moment *m.* (-e) moment; **einen - / - mal**
   just a moment
Monat *m.* (-e) month
Morgen *m.* (-) morning; **guten -** good
   morning; **morgens** in the morning
morgen tomorrow; **- früh** tomorrow
   morning
Motor *m.* (-en) engine, motor
Motorrad *n.* (¨er) motor cycle
müde tired
München Munich; **Münchner** *(adj.)*
   Munich
Mund *m.* (-e) mouth
Museum *n.* (-en) museum

müssen must, have to; **ich muß** I must
Mutter *f.* (¨) mother; **Mutti** *f.* Mum(my)
nach *(+dat.)* after, to
Nachmittag *m.* (-e) afternoon
   nachmittags in the afternoon
Nachricht *f.* (-en) message
Nachtisch *m.* (-e) dessert
nächst next
Nacht *f.* (¨e) night
nah near; **in der Nähe** in the vicinity,
   nearby
Name *m.* (-n) name
Nase *f.* (-n) nose
naß wet
natürlich naturally, of course
neben *(+ acc./dat.)* near, beside
nehmen take
nein no
nett nice
neu new
nicht not; **-s** nothing
Nieren *pl.* kidneys
nimmt: see nehmen
noch yet, again, still; **- einmal** another
   one; **-mal** again
Nord, Norden *m.* north
Normal *n.* 2-star (petrol)
Notausgang *m.* (¨e) emergency exit
Notdienst *m.* (-e) emergency service
Notfall *m.* (¨e) emergency; **im -** in an
   emergency
Nummer *f.* (-n) number
nun now
nur only

oben on top
Ober: Herr -! waiter!
Obst *n.* fruit; **-kuchen** *m.* (-) fruit pie;
   -torte *f.* (-n) fruit flan
oder or
offen open; **öffnen** *(verb)* open;
   Öffnungszeiten *pl.* opening hours
ohne *(+ acc.)* without
Ohr *n.* (-en) ear
Öl *n.* oil
Oper *f.* (-n) opera
Orangensaft *m.* (¨e) orange juice
Orchester *n.* (-) orchestra
Ordnung *f.* (-en) order; **in -** in order
Ost, Osten *m.* east

Paar *n.* (-e) pair; **ein paar** a few
Packung *f.* (-en) packet, carton
Paket *n.* (-e) packet, parcel

VOCABULARY

Panne *f.* (-n) breakdown
Papier *n.* (-e) paper
Parfüm *n.* (-e) perfume
Park *m.* (-s) park
Parkett *n.* stalls
Parkplatz *f.* (¨e) car park; Parkscheibe *f.*
   (-n) parking disc; Parkuhr *f.* (-en)
   parking meter
Party *f.* party
Paß *m.* (¨e) passport
Passant *m.* (-en) passer-by
passen fit; es paßt ohnen it fits you
passieren to happen, pass; passiert
   happened
Person *f.* (-en) person
Pfeffer *n.* pepper
Pflaster *m.* (-) sticking plaster
Pfund *n.* (-e) pound
Picknick *n.* picnic
Pille *f.* (-n) pill
Pilz *m.* (-e) mushroom
Platz *m.* (¨e) place, seat; square
Polizei *f.* police; -wache *f.* (-n) police
   station
Polizist *m.* (-en) policeman
Pommes Frites *pl.* chips
populär popular
Portmonnaie *n.* (-s) purse
Post *f.* post, post office; -amt *n.* (¨er) post
   office; -answeisung *f.* (-en) money
   order; -beamte(r)/in *m., f.* (-, innen)
   post office clerk; -fach *n.* p.o. box;
   -karte *f.* (-n) post card
präsentieren present
Preis *m.* (-e) price; preiswert good
   value
prima! great!
prüfen check, test
Puder *m.* (-) powder
Pullover *m.* (-) pullover

Quetschung *f.* (-en) bruise
Quittung *f.* (-en) receipt

Rad *n.* (¨er) wheel; -fahren *n.* cycling
Radio *n.* (-s) radio
Rang *m.* (¨e) row
Rasierapparat *m.* (-e) razor;
   Rasiercreme *f.* shaving cream;
   Rasierklingen *pl.* razor blades
raten advise
Rathaus *n.* (¨e) town hall
Raucher *m.* smoker
Raum *m.* (¨e) room

Rechner *m.* (-) calculator
Rechnung *f.* (-en) bill
recht right; rechts on the right
Regen *m.* rain; -mantel *m.* (¨) raincoat;
   regnen *(verb)* rain
Reifen *m.* (-) tyre; -druck *m.* tyre
   pressure; -panne *f.* puncture
Reis *m.* rice
Reise *f.* (-n) journey; -büro *n.* (-s) travel
   agency; -führer *m.* (-) guide book;
   -scheck *m.* (-s) traveller's cheque;
   -tasche *f.* (-n) travel bag
Rennbahn *f.* (-en) race course
Rentner/in *m., f.* (-, innen) pensioner
Reparatur *f.* (-en) repair; -werkstatt *f.*
   (¨e) repairs garage
reparieren repair
reservieren reserve; reserviert
   reserved
Restaurant *n.* (-s) restaurant
Rezept *n.* (-e) prescription
Rheinwein *m.* (-e) Rhine wine
richtig right
Richtung *f.* (-en) direction; in - in the
   direction (of)
Rindfleisch *n.* beef
Rock *m.* (¨e) skirt
rosa pink
Rosé *m.* rosé wine
rot red; Rotwein *m.* red wine
Rücken *m.* (-) back
Rückfahrkarte *f.* (-n) return ticket
Rucksack *m.* (¨e) rucksack
Ruderboot *n.* (-e) rowing boat
rufen call
Ruhetag *m.* closing day
ruhig peaceful, quiet
Ruhreier *pl.* scrambled eggs
Rundfahrt *f.* (-en) tour

Saal *m.* (Säle) room, hall
sagen say, tell; sag mal say, tell me
Sahne *f.* cream
Salat *m.* (-e) lettuce, salad; -gurke *f.* (-n)
   cucumber
Salz *n.* salt
Saxophonist *m.* saxophonist
S-Bahn *f.* suburban railway
Schachtel *f.* (-n) box
schade: wie - what a shame
Schalterbeamte(r)/in *m., f.* (-, innen)
   booking office clerk
schauen look, see
Scheck *m.* (-s) cheque; -karte *f.* (-n)
   cheque card

VOCABULARY

Scheibe *f.* (-n) slice
Scheinwerfer *m.* (-) headlight
schicken send
Schießen *n.* shooting
Schinken *m.* (-) ham
Schlaf *m.* sleep; -sack *m.* (¨e) sleeping bag; **schlafen** *(verb)* sleep
Schläger *m.* (-) racquet
Schlagsahne *f.* whipped cream
schlank slim
schlecht bad
Schlittschuhe *pl.* skates; **Schlittschuhlaufen** *n.* skating
schließen shut, close
Schloß *n.* (¨er) castle
Schlüpfer *m.* briefs
Schlüssel *m.* (-) key
schmecken taste
Schmerz *m.* (-en) pain; -mittel *n.* pain killer
Schnee *m.* snow; **schneebedeckt** snowy; **schneen** *(verb)* snow
schnell quick(ly)
Schnitzel *n.* (-) escalope
Schokolade *f.* (-n) chocolate
Scholle *f.* (-n) plaice
schon already
schön lovely, beautiful; **danke** - thanks very much; **bitte** - please, don't mention it
schrecklich dreadful
Schuh *m.* (-e) shoe, boot
Schuld *f.* (-en) fault
Schule *f.* (-n) school
schwanger pregnant
schwarz black; **Schwarzbrot** *m.* rye bread; **Schwarzwald** *m.* Black Forest
Schweinefleisch *n.* pork
Schwester *f.* (-) sister
Schwimmbad *n.* (¨er) swimming bath
schwimmen swim
See *f.* (-n) sea; - *m.* (-n) lake; -zunge *f.* (-n) sole
sehen see, look
Sehenswürdigkeit *f.* (-en) sights
sehr very, very much
Seife *f.* (-n) soap
sein *(verb)* be; - *(adj.)* his, its
seit *(+ dat.)* since
Seite *f.* (-n) side; page
Sekretärin *f.* (-innen) secretary
Sekunde *f.* (-n) second
Selbstbedienung *f.* self-service
Semmeln *pl.* rolls

senden send
Senf *m.* mustard
Sessellift *m.* (-e) chairlift
sicherlich surely, of course
sie she, her; they them
Sie you
sind: *see* **sein**
singen sing
Sitzplatz *m.* (¨e) seat (travel)
Ski *m.* (-er) ski; -fahren *n.* skiing; -gelände *f.* ski grounds; -lehrer *m.* ski instructor; -schuhe/-stiefel *pl.* ski boots; -stock *m.* (¨e) ski stick
so so; **soviel** so much, many
sobald as soon as
sofort straight away
Sohn *m.* (¨e) son
sollen have to, ought, should
Sommer *m.* summer
Sonne *f.* (-n) sun; -nbrand *m.* sunburn; -nschirm *m.* (-e) sunshade
sonnig sunny
sonst: - **noch etwas?** anything else?
Sorge: machen Sie sich keine -n don't worry
Sparkasse *f.* (-n) savings bank
spät late
Spaziergang *m.* (¨e) walk; **einen** - **machen** go for a walk
Speck *m.* bacon
Speisekarte *f.* (-n) menu
Speiseöl *n.* cooking oil
Speisezimmer *n.* (-) dining room
Spezialität *f.* (-en) speciality
Spiegel *m.* (-) mirror; -ei *n.* (-er) fried egg
Spiel *n.* (-e) game play; **spielen** *(verb)* play
Sport *m.* sport; - **treiben** be keen on sport; -art *f.* (-en) (type of) sport; -zentrum *n.* (-tren) sports centre
sprechen speak
Stadion *n.* (-ien) stadium
Stadt *f.* (¨e) town; -fest *n.* (-e) town festival; -mitte *f.* town centre; -plan *m.* (¨e) town plan; -rundfahrt *f.* (-en) city tour
städtisch *(adj.)* town
stark strong
Station *f.* (-en) stop, station
stattfinden take place
Stimme *f.* (-n) voice
stimmt; das - that's right
Stock *m.* (¨e) stick; -werk *n.* (-e) storey, floor

Storch *m.* (¨e) stork
Strand *m.* (¨e) beach
Straße *f.* (-n) street; -nbahn *f.* (-en) tram
Streichholz *n.* (¨er) match
Strumpf *m.* (¨e) stocking; -hose *f.* (-en) tights
Stück *n.* (-e) piece, play
Stunde *f.* (-n) hour; **stündlich** hourly
Sturm *m.* (¨e) storm
suchen look for
Süd, Süden south
Super *n.* 4-star (petrol)
Supermarkt *m.* (¨e) supermarket
Suppe *f.* (-n) soup
süß sweet
Sweatshirt *n.* (-s) sweatshirt

Tablette *f.* (-n) tablet
Tafel *f.* (-n) bar (chocolate)
Tag *m.* (-e) day; **guten - !** hello, good day!; -**esgedeck** *n.* (-e) menu of the day
täglich daily
Tal *n.* (¨er) valley
Tankstelle *f.* (-n) filling station
tanzen dance
Taschenlampe *f.* (-n) torch
Tasse *f.* (-n) cup
Taucheranzug *m.* (¨e) wet suit
Taxi *n.* (-s) taxi; -**stand** *m.* (¨e) taxi rank
Tee *m.* (-s) tea
Teigwaren *pl.* pasta
teilnehmen take part (in)
Telefon *n.* (-e) telephone; -**nummer** *f.* (-n) telephone number; -**zelle** *f.* (-n) call box; **telefonieren** *(verb)* telephone
Telegramm *n.* (-e) telegram
Temperatur *f.* (-en) temperature
Tennis *n.* tennis; -**platz** *m.* (¨e) tennis court
Termin *m.* (-e) appointment
Terrasse *f.* (-n) terrace
teuer expensive, dear
Theater *n.* (-) theatre
Tisch *m.* (-e) table
Tochter *f.* (¨) daughter
Toilette *f.* (-n) toilet
toll! great!
Tor *n.* (-e) arch, gate
Torte *f.* (-en) tart
tragen wear, carry
treffen meet
Treffpunkt *m.* (-e) meeting place

treiben: **Sport -** be keen on sport
Treppe *f.* (-n) stairs
trinken drink
trocken dry
Tschüß! goodbye! (fam.)
Tür *f.* (-en) door
Turnhalle *f.* (-n) gymnasium
Turm *m.* (¨e) tower
typisch typical

über *(+ acc./dat.)* over, above
übergeben, sich be sick
Übernachtung *f.* (-en) mit Frühstück bed and breakfast
Uhr *f.* (-en) hour, o'clock; watch, clock
um *(+ acc.)* at, around, about
umsehen, sich look round
umsteigen change
Umsteigemöglichkeit *f.* (-en) connection (train)
umwechseln change
Unfall *m.* accident
Universität *f.* (-en) university
uns *(acc./dat.)* us, to us
unser our
unten below, at the bottom
unter *(+ acc./dat.)* under, below, beneath
Unterricht *m.* (e) lessons, instruction
unterschreiben sign
Untertiteln *pl.* sub-titles
Urlaub *m.* (-e) holiday, leave; **auf -** on holiday

Vater *m.* (¨) father; **Vati** *m.* Dad
verboten forbidden
verbrannt burnt
verbringen spend (time)
Vereinigten Staaten *pl.* USA
vergessen forget
verkaufen sell; **Verkäufer/in** *m.*, *f.* (-, innen) sales assistant
Verkehr *m.* traffic; -**samt/sverein** *n.*, *m.* (¨er, -e) tourist office
verloren lost
verschieden various, different
Versicherungskosten *pl.* insurance costs
Verspätung *f.* (-en) delay; **- haben** be late
verstaucht sprained
verstehen understand
versuchen try
viel much, many

vielleicht perhaps
Viertel *n.* (-) quarter
Vollpension *f.* full board
volltanken! fill it up (petrol)
von *(+ dat.)* from, of
vor *(+ acc./dat.)* in front of, before
voraussichtlich prospective
vorn: nach - at the front
Vorsicht *f.* (-en) care; vorsichtig careful
Vorspeise *f.* (-n) hors d'œuvre, starter
vorstellen introduce
Vorstellung *f.* (-en) performance

waschen wash; -, sich get washed
Wagen *m.* (-) car
wählen dial
wahr: nicht - ? isn't it?, don't you?, etc.
während *(+ gen.)* during
Währung *f.* (-en) currency
Wald *m.* (¨e) wood, forest
Wandern *n.* hiking, walking;
   Wanderweg *m.* (-e) footpath
wann when
war: *see* sein; wäre: *see* sein
warm warm, hot
warten (auf) wait (for), expect;
Wartesaal *m.* (-säle) waiting room
warum why
was what; - für ein . . . what a . . ., what
   sort of . . .
Wasser *n.* (-) water; -hahn *m.* (¨e) tap;
   -skifahren *n.* waterskiing
Watte *f.* cotton wool
wegen *(+ gen.)* because of, on account
   of
weh: es tut mir - it hurts (me)
Wein *m.* (-e) wine; -karte *f.* (-n) wine
   list; -stube (-n) wine bar; traube *f.* (-n)
   grape, bunch of grapes
weiß white; Weißwein *m.* (-e) white
   wine
weit far, distant
welcher/e/es which, what
Welt *f.* (-en) world
wer who
werden become; *(fut. tense)*
West, Westen *m.* west
Wetter *n.* weather; -vorhersage *f.*
   weather forecast
wie how, what; - bitte? pardon?
wieder again
Wiederhören: auf - goodbye (phone)
Wiedersehen: auf - goodbye

Wien *n.* Vienna; wiener Viennese
wieviel how much, many
Wind *m.* (-e) wind; windig windy
Winter *m.* winter; -sport *m.* winter
   sports
wir we
wirken work, function
wirklich really
wissen know
wo where
Woche *f.* (-n) week
woher where from
wohin where to
wohl well
wohnen live
Wohnwagen *m.* (-) caravan
Wolke *f.* (-) cloud
wollen want
wunderbar wonderful
Wunsch *m.* (¨e) wish
wünschen wish, want
würde: *see* werden
Wurst *f.* (¨e) sausage

zahlen pay
zählen count
Zahn *m.* (¨e) tooth; -arzt *m.* (¨e) dentist;
   -bürste *f.* (-n) toothbrush; -pasta *f.*
   toothpaste
zeigen show
Zeit *f.* (-en) time
Zeitung *f.* (-en) newspaper
zelten camp; Zelt *n.* (-e) tent; -bett *n.*
   (-en) camp bed
Zimmer *n.* (-) room
Zitrone *f.* (-n) lemon
Zoll *m.* (¨e) customs
zu *(+ dat.)* to, at; too
Zucker *m.* sugar
zuerst at first
Zug *m.* (¨e) train
zum to the; - trinken? (what would you
   like) to drink?
zur to the
zurück back; -fahren go back, return;
   -gehen go back; hin und - return
   (ticket)
zusammen together
Zuschauer *m.* (-) spectator
Zuschlag *m.* supplement
Zwiebel *f.* (-n) onion
zwischen *(+ acc./dat.)* between